Committed Uncertainty in Psychotherapy

Committed Uncertainty in Psychotherapy
Essays in Honour of Peter Lomas

Edited by
Lucy King
Cambridge Society of Psychotherapy

Whurr Publishers Ltd

© 1999 Whurr Publishers Ltd
First published 1999 by
Whurr Publishers Ltd
19b Compton Terrace, London N1 2UN, England

All rights reserved. No part of this publication may be
reproduced, stored in a retrieval system, or transmitted
in any form or by any means, electronic, mechanical,
photocopying, recording or otherwise, without the
prior permission of Whurr Publishers Limited.

This publication is sold subject to the conditions that it
shall not, by way of trade or otherwise, be lent, resold,
hired out, or otherwise circulated without the
publisher's prior consent in any form of binding or
cover other than that in which it is published and
without a similar condition including this condition
being imposed upon any subsequent purchaser.

British Library Cataloguing in Publication Data
A catalogue record for this book is available from the
British Library.

ISBN 1 86156 110 5

Printed and bound in the UK by Athenaeum Press Ltd,
Gateshead, Tyne & Wear

Contents

Contributors   vii

Preface   xi

Chapter 1   1

Treating with respect and sincerity: Peter Lomas, therapist and writer
Michael Jacobs

Chapter 2   17

Interview with Peter Lomas
Sian Morgan

Chapter 3   36

Peter Lomas: therapy and 'the Outfit'
Carol Dasgupta

Chapter 4   48

Common humanity
Lucy King

Chapter 5   62

The ordinary
John Heaton

Chapter 6   79

Imagination and metaphor in the development of the trainee psychotherapist
Rosemary Randall

| **Chapter 7** | **89** |

Peter Lomas: friend and fellow writer
David Holbrook

| **Chapter 8** | **96** |

Peter Lomas and the question of science
Peter Rudnytsky

| **Chapter 9** | **108** |

Freud in perspective: the problem of seduction
Paul Roazen

| **Chapter 10** | **120** |

The limits of technique in family therapy
Eia Asen

| **Chapter 11** | **129** |

A century of psychotherapy
David Smail

| **Chapter 12** | **139** |

The importance of being Peter Lomas: social change and the ethics of psychotherapy
David Ingleby

Bibliography of books, chapters and articles by Peter Lomas	**151**
Other authors cited	**153**
Index	**159**

Contributors

Eia Asen grew up in Berlin where he studied medicine, qualifying in 1971. He moved to London in 1973 to read Social Psychology at the London School of Economics. In 1974 he started training as a psychiatrist at the Maudsley Hospital where he came across Peter Lomas whose early books inspired him so much that he asked him to be his psychotherapist. Working full time for the NHS, partly as a Consultant Child Psychiatrist at the Malborough Family Service in North London, and partly as an Adult Consultant Psychiatrist at the Maudsley Hospital in South London, he has done research on eating disorders, depression and child abuse and has written three books, the last one being *Family Therapy for Everyone* (1995) which was launched simultaneously with a 6-part BBC series on Family Therapy.

Carol Dasgupta was a student with the Outfit from 1993 to 1997, having previously trained as a counsellor at the University of Santa Clara, California, and the University of Cambridge Counselling Service. She has worked as a Play Therapist for the NHS and at present works as a child counsellor at the Cambridge Family Divorce Centre, and as a counsellor at the University of Cambridge Counselling Service. She also works as a therapist with children, adolescents and adults in private practice.

John Heaton qualified in medicine at Cambridge University. He worked as an eye surgeon for some years and then did research at the Institute of Ophthalmology, London. After training in psychoanalytic psychotherapy he worked with R.D. Laing at the Philadelphia Association of which he became a member. He is a founder member of the Guild of Psychotherapists and was Chair of the Medical Section of the British Psychological Society. He practices in London as a psychotherapist. He is author of *The Eye: Phenomenology and Psychology of Function and Disorder*, *Metis: Divination, Psychotherapy and Cunning Intelligence* and *Wittgenstein for Beginners*; and many articles on ophthalmology, psychotherapy and philosophy.

David Holbrook is an Emeritus Fellow of Downing College, Cambridge, where he was Director of English Studies 1982–9. He has published over forty books, including poetry, novels, musical and literary criticism and studies in philosophical anthropology. His latest works include *Getting It Wrong With Uncle Tom*, *a Norfolk idyll*, *Wuthering Heights: a Dream of Being*, *Tolstoy*, *Woman and Death*, and a new collection of poems which is to appear early in 1999.

David Ingleby began his career working as a research psychologist for the Medical Research Council and subsequently taught in Social and Political Sciences at Cambridge University. In this time he participated in the setting up by Peter Lomas and others of the Outfit, for training therapists. In 1982 he moved to Holland to take up a chair in Developmental Psychology at Utrecht University. His current activities include research on the mental health needs of asylum-seekers, refugees and other migrants. His publications include *Critical Psychiatry: The politics of mental health* (Penguin 1981) and numerous articles on psychology, psychiatry and psychoanalysis.

Lucy King trained as a biologist but after several years of research, abandoned the microscope in favour of a more people-orientated occupation. She trained first as a counsellor, and then as a psychoanalytic psychotherapist with the Philadelphia Association. She is a founder member of the Cambridge Society for Psychotherapy. She is a course tutor on Cambridge University's Advanced Diploma in Counselling, works for the Cambridge University Counselling Service and as a psychotherapist in private practice.

Michael Jacobs is Director of the Counselling and Psychotherapy Certificate Programme in the Department of Adult Education, Leicester University. He is a Fellow of the British Association of Counselling and a UKCP registered psychotherapist. He has written a number of books on counselling and related subjects, including some key textbooks used in training courses throughout Britain including *The Presenting Past*, *Psychodynamic Counselling in Action*, *Still Small Voice*, and *Swift to Hear*. He has written on two Key Figures in the Sage series, *Sigmund Freud*, and *D.W. Winnicott*, and he is a Consultant Editor with the Open University Press for the psychotherapy and counselling list.

Sian Morgan is an analytic psychotherapist working in private practice in Cambridge. She trained at the Guild of Psychotherapists and has been a member of the Cambridge Society for Psychotherapy since 1989. She is a book review editor for the European Journal of Psychotherapy and is currently editing a book on phobias. She teaches psychodynamic counselling and is interested in contributing to and encouraging the development of psychotherapy and counselling in the public sector, particularly within the maternity services.

Rosemary Randall is a psychotherapist working in private practice. She has a degree in English Literature and trained in group work and counselling while working for mental health services in London in the 1970's. During this period she was involved in various political, feminist and co-operative groups and co-authored the cartoon book *The Barefoot Psychoanalyst*. She later worked as a lecturer at the Open University and as a freelance writer. She joined the Cambridge Society for Psychotherapy in 1983 as one of its first trainees, graduating in 1989, and had remained closely involved in the development of the Society and its work.

Paul Roazen was a professor of Social and Political Science at York University in Toronto. He is an eminent writer on Freud and the history of the psychoanalytic movement. His books include: *Freud and his Followers, Meeting Freud's Family,* and *Freud: Political and Social Thought.*

Peter Rudnytsky is Professor of English at the University of Florida and a corresponding Member of the Institute of Contemporary Psychoanalysis in Los Angeles. He is the author of *Freud and Oedipus* (1997) and *The Psychoanalytic Vocation: Rank, Winnicott and the Legacy of Freud* (1991), and the the editor of *Transitional Objects and Potential Spaces: Literary Uses of D.W. Winnicott* (1993).

David Smail, formerly head of clinical psychology services in Nottingham, has recently retired from work in the NHS. He has for many years been Special Professor in Clinical Psychology at Nottingham University and is author of several books on psychological therapy, most recently *How to Survive Without Psychotherapy* (1996).

Preface

This collection of essays has been compiled as a tribute to the work of the psychotherapist, Peter Lomas, who celebrated his 75th birthday earlier this year.

Peter trained as a Freudian psychoanalyst at the Institute of Psycho-analysis in London. Gradually, however, he became more heterodox in his views about both the practice of psychotherapy and the training of psychotherapists, and he eventually parted company with the Institute and the British Psycho-analytic Society. As is made clear in his writings and through the pages of this volume, his approach to psychotherapy rejects the ideal of the neutral analytic stance in favour of a more direct interpersonal dialogue in which he is much more prepared to be emotionally open and to own up to his human frailties than are most therapists within the analytic tradition. This approach has led him to be regarded as something of a maverick by more orthodox analysts. On the other hand, a great many people have been touched by his courage, honesty and openness, which they have found inspiring and helpful.

It is somehow typical of Peter Lomas's anti-institutional style that the training organization that he co-founded in Cambridge should have become widely known, even outside its own membership, by the jokingly proposed non-name, 'the Outfit'. It later acquired a 'proper' title, 'the Cambridge Society for Psychotherapy', but 'the Outfit' has stuck.

The contibutors to this book comprise friends and colleagues who are broadly sympathetic to his criticisms of mainstream psychoanalysis, and others more directly or profoundly influenced by him – as patients, pupils, readers and fellow therapists. The book opens with an introduction to Peter Lomas's work by Michael Jacobs. This is followed by an interview with him conducted by Sian Morgan. The next two chapters (Carol Dasgupta and Lucy King) are reflections upon personal experiences of therapy and training with him. Then follow six chapters that comment on aspects of Peter Lomas's work, or on psychoanalysis and psychotherapy from points of view sympathetic to his. The final two chapters (David Smail and David Ingleby) place Peter Lomas' work in a historical and social context.

As well as to Peter Lomas himself, the main credit for this book belongs to Dr Ved Varma. It was his initiative and his hard work that got the project under way. I took over the editorship only when Dr Varma became ill over the summer of 1997 and felt unable to complete the work. I am grateful to him for all the arduous groundwork he carried out and for his continuing support.

Lucy King
Cambridge
December 1998

Chapter 1
Treating with respect and sincerity: Peter Lomas, therapist and writer

MICHAEL JACOBS

Psychoanalysis is an enthralling discipline, but it can also hold in thrall: it sometimes seems all-embracing, but it can smother those caught in its embrace. Peter Lomas is one of several eminent writers and therapists who have wrested themselves free of the more crippling aspects of psychoanalysis, particularly in his native Britain, but who also keeps us fascinated by its ideas and processes. Unlike some of those who have turned both their back and their vengeance upon their parent body, Lomas combines trenchant criticism of the theory, the practice and the institution that is psychoanalysis with discriminating acknowledgement of what he thinks is right about all three elements. It is worth noting at the outset that Lomas has said that if under pressure ('if . . . a gun was held at my head!')[1] he would call himself a Freudian. Indeed it is his adhesion to these roots that makes him both so interesting, and so important. He is not an analyst gone soft.

One of the aspects of psychoanalysis that Lomas continues to value is the significance of the past (if anything, giving the past a stronger reality than some analysts do in the triumph of fantasy over experience), so it is legitimate to trace the influences, both personal and intellectual, that have led and fed Lomas in his professional career as a therapist and a writer. We might expect, for example, that several years as a general practitioner before his training at the Institute of Psychoanalysis, London, would give him a somewhat different outlook on ordinary human suffering at the outset of that training. Many of his fellow analysands would have specialized more in psychiatry or psychology. That grounding in the public health service, including at one time working as director of a child-guidance clinic, gave Lomas (like Winnicott) experience of a wider range of people than is often the case in the 'élite' circle of privileged patients and analysts associated with the Institute. His first major book, *True and False Experience*, is 'a record of my attempt to escape from the obscurities of a speciality into the common light of day' (Lomas, 1973: 19) – perhaps back to that early experience of the common light of day in his early years as a doctor. It is not surprising that Lomas became critical of traditional psychoanalysis relatively quickly, even if he kept fairly quiet about it in print, as his training analyst was Charles Rycroft, at that time a member of the 'Independent Group' (neither purist Freudians or Kleinians) and one who, like Lomas, has since withdrawn from membership of the British Psycho-analytic Society. Rycroft encouraged his analysand to think for himself. Supervision by Marion Milner can only have strengthened that independent spirit, as would experiences during his training such as at the Cassel Hospital – an avant-garde therapeutic community – his friendship and work at one time with R D Laing, and his first-hand acquaintance with Winnicott.

As a student Peter Lomas was somewhat disenchanted with the dogmatism and narrowness of psychoanalysis, although he remains deeply grateful to Freud, and in various places in his writing he lists influences upon him such as Jung, Ferenczi, Erikson, Winnicott and Rycroft and from the United States, Searles – 'among the most creative in the literature' (Lomas, 1987b: 120) – and Bateson. Lomas particularly values Winnicott's concepts of the true and false self, although he is also critical of Winnicott, especially for not applying the same facilitating environment to therapy as a whole that he used with especially regressed patients. Lomas's own thinking about the therapist and the task of therapy has clearly been influenced by the idea of the emergence of the true self (Lomas, 1973: 7). He has also been inspired by the writings of Buber, Kierkegaard and the existential school, as well as excited by the studies of 'schizophrenogenic' families. Although some have seen him as a crypto-Rogerian, he was in fact introduced to the parallels with the founder of the person-centred tradition after he had framed his own criticisms of psychoanalysis, and he has his own qualifications to make of that important contribution to practice. He refers widely as well as critically to psychoanalytic theory, particularly valuing the existential perspective, and he draws upon a wide range of literary sources, as well as upon clinical examples from his own private practice. This setting has given him the freedom to work in what he believes is the best interests of his patients, so that although private work has gone against his principles of social justice, 'the researcher in me has won the day' (private communication, 1998).

Lomas has clearly either sought out or been attracted to the more independent thinkers in the psychoanalytic and psychotherapeutic world. This life-long energetic drive to be free to think for himself, and to encourage others to do so, may be a positive reaction against a childhood upbringing that was loving yet restricting. Ironically, he was drawn to training with a similarly restrictive parent body, and as indicated below has been compelled several times in his professional career to repeat the escape from unnecessary and rigid confinements. In this he has been influenced and supported by his wife Diana, whom he regards as quicker than he in seeing through the pretensions of theory.

His early papers, many of which are re-printed in *Personal Disorder and the Family* (1998), hint at what follows later, more explicitly and more cogently argued, in a series of books that question many of the assumptions of traditional psychoanalysis. Above all Lomas promotes the centrality of the therapeutic relationship as a model for the best of human relationships. The different elements of his approach are examined below, although historically it is interesting to observe that in his first (and only) book as an editor of one of the Institute's own publications, Lomas's opening essay plunges straight into the necessity in therapy of looking for the whole person, and not for external improvements to a machine. He upbraids psychology for fragmenting the person 'into a collection of drives, quotients and body parts' (Lomas, 1967: 9). If Lomas in this essay still accepts and justifies the artificiality of psychoanalysis – such as the couch, and that ordinary happenings in social intercourse are avoided – he nevertheless stresses the experience and understanding of the personal relationship between the therapist and patient as being vitally important. He notes that psychiatry and psychoanalysis have tended to see the patient's view as at worst meaningless or at best unbalanced and exaggerated, and 'the patient's capacity for accurate perception [as] . . . marked down' (Lomas, 1967a: 12). This advocacy of the good standing of the patient (and indeed of the patient's unconscious) is one of his most important later contributions.

It is fascinating, at this distance from that early publication, to note Lomas's list of the ways in which a family does not meet a child's needs and to ask whether these points anticipate his later views on what a patient tends to get from the standard psychoanalytic practice:

1. the child is not given reliably affectionate fondling to satisfy sensuous needs
2. his picture of reality is confused in the way it is presented to him by others
3. his capacity to express and receive emotional experience is dulled or crushed by discouraging responses
4. no clear path of development is marked out for him, no suitable leader exists on whom he can model himself. (Lomas, 1967a: 17–18)

Towards the end of the essay he concludes that 'a general improvement in psychological health can only be expected if and when children grow up in families in which they are treated with respect and sincerity as real and unique persons' (Lomas, 1967a: 24). Substitute patients for children, and therapy for families, and this is the key to Peter Lomas's practice. It is also the key to his writing. As one reviewer wrote: 'The author communicated great respect for the reader's intelligence, sophistication and humanity; judging from Lomas's wonderful clinical examples, it is the same attitude he communicates to his patients' (Roth, 1994: 1299–300).

Within a few years Lomas had become more outspoken, and could no longer tolerate the narrowness of the Institute. The response to his first major book, *True and False Experience*, was a rather obvious silence within the psychoanalytic community: it was never reviewed in any of the main journals, although he received considerable appreciation from his wider readership. He resigned his membership of the Institute in 1974, and went on with others to found the Guild of Psychotherapists in London. Disillusioned, too, with the way that organization developed, he resigned from it in 1978, and in 1981 became a founder member of the Cambridge Society for Psychotherapy, where he is still an active member. However, unhappy still at having to be trapped by labels, such as the 'psychoanalytic' tag that has to be fixed to the Society in order to be affiliated to the UK Council for Psychotherapy, Lomas has since 1997 decided not to remain a registered member.

The psychoanalytic heritage

Lomas sees Freud as essential, although he recognizes (of course) that it is possible to be a psychotherapist without being Freudian (Lomas, 1981: 19). In a letter in the *International Review of Psychoanalysis* he vigorously states that 'a psychotherapist who ignores the precious insights given to us by Freud would be grievously mistaken in doing so' (Lomas, 1985: 361). Amongst a number of indications of this homage, Lomas writes that Freud constructed an impressive intellectual edifice, that he gave people attention, that he encouraged patients to take responsibility for themselves, that he took little for granted, and that he always looked beneath the surface (Lomas, 1981: 19). He implies agreement with Freud's use of a conversation as a method, with free association, the recognition of defences and transference, and the space, time and freedom of the psychoanalytic session; with the significance of early childhood; that people are physical and they have bodies; that love and hate are wild passions that cannot be repressed without cost; that failure to establish sexual identity is crippling; that people adapt to society with painful loss of potential; that conflicts are expressed in language (dreams as well) whose structure has a different logic from conscious thought; and that people use fantasy as a defence (Lomas, 1973: 58–60).

There are inevitably limitations in Freud's theory, and Lomas singles out in particular his excessive rationality, a mechanical and bio-physical theory, his underestimation of the adult in the patient (as he similarly points to Rogers's neglect of the child in the adult), and an excessive preoccupation with the past. Being a Freudian is too easily equated with being an atheist and a pessimist, which Lomas is not. But above all what Lomas criticizes is not Freud himself, but that type of thinking that 'freezes people into Freudian, existential or any other blocks of ice' (Lomas, 1968a: 116)

If Lomas simply pointed to excesses or weaknesses in Freudian theory, he would be of little interest. He does more than this as he, by and large, accepts familiar concepts, such as interpretations, defences and transference, but moves beyond a narrow or singular use of them in practice, enlarging the possibilities both for the therapeutic interaction, and for understanding the patient.

The limits of interpretation

Lomas does not like the reductionism of many psycho-analytic interpretations. Indeed he entitles one of his books *The Limits of Interpretation*. Part of his criticism is aimed at the over-precise, and artificial way of using words, which Lomas sees as evidence of a defensive tendency on the part of the therapist: for example, 'you seem to be thinking of me as though I were an over-protective mother' (Lomas, 1973: 140). He is certainly not averse to a careful choice of words: but that is different from being inhibited. Patients can be confused by some analytic communication; and it is little wonder, Lomas observes, that patients resort to the kind of unconscious communication that Robert Langs identifies, because the therapeutic relationship is such that they cannot directly communicate their disappointment at the failings in their therapist (Lomas, 1987b: 123).

A different type of inhibition occurs when interpretation is over-influenced by psychoanalytic theory because this does not allow enough space for the patient's material to form into its own interpretation. Therapists also tend to concentrate on what they think and speak, without giving adequate acknowledgement to the way they act: everything a therapist does, as well as says, is a type of interpretation. What is the overall message that therapists give, in their manner as well as their words? The therapist's silence and neutrality, the adoption of the 'blank screen' provides its own message, and indeed may convey an arrogant use of power that is anything but neutral. Analysts actually argue that their abstinence deliberately seeks to evoke, through frustration, long repressed feelings or needs. Lomas does not believe that this is the only way of evoking feelings and needs, suggesting instead that building up trust, and modelling a different type of relationship from that experienced by the patient in the past, is just as likely to promote them. It is better to regress out of hope than out of frustration with the blank screen. In that sense he anticipates the identification of the developmentally needed relationship as a significant aspect of the therapeutic alliance, although his avowal of the corrective emotional experience is at the same time a theme that he acknowledges he inherits from Ferenczi, Rank, and Alexander and French. Lomas does not advocate so relaxed a milieu that there is no anxiety. By being facilitating but not over-protective, the therapist may allow trusting exposure of wounds and 'the arousal of hope and the motivation needed for healing' (Lomas, 1981: 61). In one of a number of comments that show that Lomas is not always convinced by other forms of therapy either, he doubts that this type of caring can be accomplished adequately through a deliberate planned attempt to behave in a warm and nurturing manner (Lomas, 1987b: 81).

There is a danger in psychoanalysis of interpreting a patient's defences as being against the reality of the therapist's interpretations. In fact, Lomas believes successful treatment may be more because of the therapist's encouragement of the patient's potentiality, which has been criticized or crushed previously in the patient's life: 'The interpretations of the patient's defence and the technical procedures which figure so much in the literature of psychotherapy will play far less a part than a personal relationship which permits and encourages spontaneity and growth' (Lomas, 1973: 120). The tendency in psychoanalysis is to concentrate upon a patient's defences – upon their unwillingness to get in touch with their unconscious wishes – rather than on the confusion that the patient has experienced and is still experiencing. In those circumstances to concentrate upon defences is to risk making the patient even more confused, the therapist becoming somewhat like the schizophrenogenic mother. What a therapist needs to do is to pay more attention to the way in which people have become confused, rather than confuse them further with what for the patient is an enigmatic technique.

Transference

There are places where Lomas shows suspicion of transference interpretations, as examples of a defence used by analysts against their fright at powerful feelings in the patient, and against too deep an emotional involvement with their patients. It was, of course, such an experience that pushed Freud into an understanding of transference, without properly acknowledging his own part in the situation (Freud, 1925: 210–11). Lomas acknowledges transference as central to Freud's work, but he questions the way transference is normally identified as an inappropriate reaction to the present, which must therefore have its origins elsewhere. It may be feelings from the past that are experienced in the present; but if the present provokes them, how can we be sure that they only come from the past? He argues that what is called 'transference' can also be an appropriate reaction to the actual situation of therapy, even if it is probably combined with an element of past experience. Therefore the lack of response by a therapist is likely of itself to evoke anger, hurt, withdrawal, confusion, idealization and envy in the patient, and there need not always be antecedents to produce such a transference (Lomas, 1973: 139). For example, a therapist is not just a symbolic figure; he or she is also a sexual being. Lomas provides an example of a patient whose sexual dreams, unconsciously expressing her wishes for that type of relationship with him as therapist, were not just transference. Although there were incestuous implications in her father's provocative behaviour, they were also about the temptations of the intimacy that therapy (if of any depth) almost always involves (Lomas, 1981: 56–8). The delicate way in which he handles this example is also an illustration of what Lomas means when he writes of the need to choose words carefully. He does not suggest that spontaneity or openness in the therapist involves an 'unthinking precipitate response' (Lomas, 1981: 78).

Furthermore, Lomas observes that an 'inappropriate' transference can take place even when therapists permit themselves to relate in ordinary and natural ways with the client. While it may have once been necessary to adopt the clinical purity of the laboratory in therapy, in order to identify the phenomenon and to study it, transference is now so much part of our understanding of relationships (outside therapy as much as within it), that we do not need to have to use an extraordinary procedure in order to maximise it or use it (Lomas, 1973: 138). In fact we might argue that inappropriate reactions are more likely to be true transference if they appear for no apparent reason, unconnected with the therapist's behaviour, than if they have been engineered through the apparent neutrality of traditional analytic technique.

Lomas is never afraid to use extensive illustrations from his own work, and he reproduces a lengthy interchange in one chapter whereby he shows that in this particular session it was not necessary to interpret the transference for positive therapeutic developments to take place in the patient (Lomas, 1981: 67–79). He provides in his receptivity and openness what was missing for the patient in her own childhood: open and honest communication; but he also illustrates with exactly the same patient that when it is useful he will make interpretations of a more standard kind. He reports a later interchange where 'I found myself making an interpretation in the "classical" Freudian manner' (Lomas, 1981: 95–6), although the way in which he expresses his interpretation is straightforward and still clearly personal. Lomas would not have psychoanalytic therapists neglect the transference interpretation, but rather would have them extend the range of their interventions to include a variety of responses, which their rigid training has led them to consider too dangerous for the patient or to the therapeutic relationship.

Lomas turns accepted wisdom on its head: whereas it is often thought in analytic circles that the therapist's more personal remarks are likely to provoke inappropriate reactions in the patient, and to intensify the erotic transference, he argues that *frustration* is more likely to produce such a result, and that more natural responses will lead to more natural relating. This is reminiscent of Ferenczi's note, that 'it is my fault that the transference has become so passionate – as a result of my *coldness*. A much too literal repetition of the father-daughter dependence: *promises* (forepleasure, gratifications, leading to expectations) and then nothing given' (Ferenczi, 1955: 262 – Ferenczi's emphases).

Lomas acknowledges that the concepts of transference and countertransference help therapists 'keep a balanced mind in the face of their patients' demand that they respond in a certain (and often misguided) way' (Lomas, 1997b: 128), but he highlights through various references in his writing two major contradictions or confusions. One confusion is that psychoanalytic technique is not sure what to do about the transference: sometimes it wants to develop the transference by heightening the patient's feelings, in order to see them at first hand within the therapeutic relationship; in other situations the guidelines for technique dictate that the analyst must avoid behaviours and interventions that might provoke strong feelings in the patient, because they are too much for the therapist or the patient to handle. Lomas identifies another contradiction (although it may also be his own): in one chapter in *True and False Experience* he thinks that therapists are too modest to claim that a patient is helped by 'my warmth, integrity, courage, strength, sensitivity, realism, honesty', saying instead 'It's the technique' (Lomas, 1973: 135); later in the same book he suggests that therapists, like government, take gratitude and love as rewards for their efforts, but criticism as the product of negative transference. It is as if therapists are often uncertain what to make either of themselves or of their patients' reactions.

The good therapist

Lomas is very critical of the term 'technique': it is inappropriate for use in a situation where his premiss is that each person is unique and unpredictable. As indicated above, the emergence of the transference and the need to understand defences do not require the traditional blank screen. Indeed, more may be achieved through the therapist being authentic. Lomas's 'philosophy of living' is that it is better to be in communication with people than to be withdrawn (Lomas, 1973: 14). Rather than simply interpret the negative, whether it is patients' defensiveness or their neurotic transference, therapists should model the positive – and they certainly do not have to *explain* everything. Psychotherapy is not so much about treating the sick but rather about finding a way through false ways of living; and if therapy is about the patient finding a true sense of self and life, the therapist must be real. The patient needs to be able to make an impact upon the therapist – 'giving, caring, criticizing' (Lomas, 1987b: 119); and therapist has to expose self to risk of 'ridicule, rejection, criticism' (Lomas, 1987b: 131). We have to risk disillusionment of the therapist and the patient, so that they can come closer to each other.

In certain circumstances Winnicott advocates a departure from anything that could be called a technique. Lomas similarly illustrates that on occasion (normally when a patient is particularly distressed) he can adapt his manner. At the end of *True and False Experience* he provides a long example, where some sessions are held outside in the garden, where he allows the patient to hold on to him; then he takes her hand; and later accepts her questions about him for two sessions, during which time he reveals some of his deepest anxieties. It is these occasions (which are not frequent in his practice, but which do illustrate the extent to which he will try to respond authentically), that have given rise to considerable criticism of him. Lomas believes that much that goes under the name of technique prevents therapists from engaging in this kind of authentic relationship. His justification for what might be called departures from standard technique is that in this way he enables the patient to see him as real. In this particular example his sensitivity to the patient's needs in therapy was, he believes. instrumental in helping to contain her deep fear of disintegration. But he is also clear that these actions are only of value if they are not contrived.

The task of therapy is to reveal both possibility and limitation. Lomas obviously opens up more possibilities for relating than traditional training permits, but he also is quite aware of the necessity for limitations to be made clear to therapist and patient. He accepts, for example, that it is difficult to distinguish the subtle difference between true and false experience – what looks like openness might be collusion, or mutual narcissism (Lomas, 1981: 77). He is himself deeply critical of the power of the therapist. When he writes that 'eminent practitioners have ruthlessly used their status to ensure that their theories are accepted' (Lomas, 1997b: 129), he would obviously include less eminent practitioners in this comment. The two greatest temptations are to exploit a patient through intellectual and sexual domination. 'It is clearly the duty of the therapist to ensure that he does not harm the patient by seduction, flirtation, or overtly sexual behavior' (Lomas, 1997b: 129). The power of the therapist should maximize the patient's autonomy, and not diminish the patient's 'natural intuition and wisdom' (Lomas, 1994: 13). Power can of course be misused in a number of ways: not only is Lomas critical of the coerciveness of (for example) Kleinian methods, but also of the 'gentle approach characteristic of some schools of thought' (Lomas, 1987b: 101), the seductively as well as the aggressively powerful therapies.

Lomas is deeply aware of the disasters that can arise from abuse by therapists. If when reading of some of his departures from standard practice and therapist 'neutrality' any should doubt the high standards

Lomas sets himself and therapists generally, it is important to note a growing interest, in his more recent writing, in the moral life of the therapist. In addition to spelling out the value of the personal and the ordinary against reliance on specialized theory and technique, he focuses on morality in the sense the ancient Greeks used the term, to refer to the matter of living a good life rather than to the more narrow contemporary conception of the judgement of right and wrong. He is essentially now wanting to discuss *mores*, ways of being, which is not the same as ethical dilemmas. In the context of therapy this means the way a therapist is with the patient.

Lomas titles his contribution to one edited book 'The Moral Maze of Psychoanalysis'. He observes that psychoanalysis has thrown up some who can be called geniuses, but these people have been idealized by their followers, and that there have been times when ruthless competition, shabby treatment of colleagues, and lack of confidentiality has fallen short of the standards expected of therapists. There has been a conspiracy in the psychoanalytic establishment to conceal the truth about the behaviour of some of its heroes, to promote the movement as the product of wise, responsible and competent men, who have maturity to approach their material impartially. While Lomas emphasizes that a therapist must behave morally, in a way that a laboratory scientist does not have to, he also believes that there is an arrogance in some psychoanalytic writing that is very pertinent to these wider issues of morality.

Lomas says that to write as a therapist about the value of love, humility, or spontaneity can easily be seen as sentimental, intellectually sloppy and arrogant. Nevertheless he is certain that the wise therapist who seeks to heal will reveal qualities we normally reckon to be 'good': wisdom, love, patience, honesty, warmth, closeness, trust, encouragement, spontaneity and intuition.[2] He makes no claims to be any 'better' than other therapists in this respect, but he does claim that, unlike many of them, he is ready to acknowledge the importance of these qualities for healing, and the central role they play in developing and practising the therapeutic attitude.

It is important to remember that Lomas was deeply involved with research into mothers and babies. Like Winnicott, he emphasizes the need for therapists to function in a maternal way, whereas analytic therapy tends to emphasize masculine qualities such as discipline, reticence, toughness and control (Lomas, 1987b: 79). Psychoanalysis is often paternalistic when it needs to be maternal. In one context Lomas sees friendship as the paradigm for psychotherapy (1981: 6). Patients will be helped if the therapist and patient grow to like, understand, respect each other: 'It is not something that I was led to expect by my training; rather it is a truth that has painfully been forced upon me by earlier failure' (Lomas, 1973: 133).

The truthful patient

Psychoanalytic case-studies, and sometimes supervision, to all intents and purposes write or speak of many patients as devious and difficult: as shrinking away from the truth, as being defensive, and as having memories that deny their complicity through their own fantasies. The impression is given, and is probably acted upon in practice (even if denied in theory), that patients are unhelpful and uncooperative and that it is the task of the analyst to provide a milieu which will break down the patient's deep defences.

Lomas puts forward a very different perspective on the motivation and the honesty of the patient. He believes that the patient is pursuing truth at least as much as avoiding it, and that Freud underestimates the desire of the patient to find the truth. A person's capacity to search for or accept the truth must be recognized and encouraged.

The two theories of origin of mental illness – that it is defence (on the side of the adult) or confusion (on the side of the child) – are both unsatisfactory for the practice of psychotherapy. The internalization of parental figures in the course of ordinary development (as they were perceived rather than as they were) has also been exaggerated, so that insufficient notice is taken of the actual parents in real life. Lomas is convinced of the need to look for the truth about childhood experience (as, for example, in abuse) and that the closest we can get to the true situation is through what is happening in therapy. He is critical of the dominant psychoanalytic view that mental disturbance comes from the internal conflicts over infantile urges, rather than allowing for what parents were really like, or were perceived to be like. Here again, truth – and the difference between narrative truth and historical truth – is essential. It is not enough to engage in a 'fairy story' that has coherence, and therefore soothes even when it is not true. Lomas makes it clear that patients are desperate to be believed, and to have someone who will affirm their view of the way things were, if indeed that is the way it seems to the therapist.

In needing a therapist who believes in them, patients also need a therapist who will provide (in the words of Medard Boss (1963), whom Lomas cites) 'the opportunity to live and to experience, over and over again, immediately and unreflectingly, their new ways of behaviour within the safe relationship to the analyst' (Lomas, 1973: 85–6). The patient is seeking a 'second, late, attempt to unfold his true self' (Lomas, 1973: 87), and this is one of the key issues of psychotherapeutic endeavour.

In this sense Lomas, although taking this idea of the true self from Winnicott, shares something of the humanistic optimism in the natural process of growth and development inherent in each human being. He believes that psychoanalysis (whether in traditional Freudian form or in the more radical theories of R D Laing) is too pessimistic in its view of human relationships, and may only confirm a patient's view that love does not exist. At the same time Lomas has more than enough clinical experience to know that patients can sometimes be extraordinarily difficult to work with, and he describes how 'some of the most painful experiences I have suffered are occasions when I have given my heart to a patient only to find that the sincerity of my behaviour had been understood by him as a triumph of his manipulative power' (Lomas, 1981: 144).

Training for therapy

Lomas finds himself in something of a dilemma: he does not wish to become the expert or guru, whom others will idealize, and in the process diminish their own capacity to find their particular way of being a therapist. He wants, however, to liberate practising therapists both from the self-imposed shackles of their techniques and from a training for therapy that depends upon modelling upon a system or a person. He believes that it takes at least 10 years to distance oneself from such a training and to learn to be oneself.

Nevertheless he has had to provide the leadership to show that it is possible both to practise as a therapist and to train as a therapist in a different way. This he has done in founding new training groups. He has never wished to found a particular school of opinion or of technique, but rather a way of training that will enhance all that is best in therapeutic practice, and that above all, encourages therapists to find, and work with, what is most authentic. A major part of that training involves helping the student therapist look at the false ways he or she behaves towards people (Lomas, 1973: 18).

He sees no reason to have a medical training in order to practise as a therapist. He is also concerned that the expense of training is crippling, and he is critical of the élitism of which money is a part. A good training involves the opportunity to learn about oneself; to learn about people from the experience of seeing them; and to improve one's intuitive response. Being with disturbed people, and supervision of early work are also key elements. Personal therapy is essential, but requiring it, and laying down its frequency, and reporting on its progress (as is typical of most psychotherapy trainings at least in regards to the first two aspects) militates against the effectiveness of this experience. While the contradictions here are clear (essential, but should not be required) what Lomas is getting at (in training and in the practice of therapy) is that essentially it is the spirit that matters, rather than the letter. Good training needs to encourage students to take responsibility for themselves, in relation to their personal development and in terms of the acquisition of knowledge. He suggests, nevertheless, that part of the knowledge base should be attention to a realistic history of the psychoanalytic movement, and to issues that may have led therapists to adopt particular (often discourteous) approaches, such as abstinence as a way of revealing the unconscious.

If therapy involves, above all, what Lomas calls the 'ordinary human response' (Lomas, 1973: 15), what is special about therapists? They are, he says elsewhere, ordinary human beings like mothers, social workers, clergy – and what their training does is to increase their capacity to be ordinary human beings. What makes them different is that they focus on the patient; and they are experienced at treating sick people, although their skills are not esoteric. Their training should have revealed the different ways therapists can fail to be true and ordinary to themselves (Lomas, 1973: 137). Lomas is not simplistically identifying a good therapist with someone who is well meaning. He may reject technique but he still advocates rigour: for example, he compares listening to the patient to close attention to the text in literary criticism (Lomas, 1981: 11). It may be debated whether therapy is a science or an art (although he makes it clear that the 'scientific' label is not one he favours), but perhaps it is better to see therapy as a craft. In addition to knowledge, and to experience in the work, Lomas also values immensely the life experience that any trainee therapist brings. He stresses the necessity of ordinary human qualities.

The weakness in Lomas's equation of the therapist with the ordinary person is that, although he does spell out the qualities that he would have the therapist show, these are far from ordinary; or perhaps far from normal. When, for example, Lomas cites himself saying to a patient, 'I need you to stop keeping away from me' (Lomas, 1973: 13) this is not an ordinary or a normal response to someone who keeps their distance. Most people would either say nothing, but distance themselves in turn, or perhaps become angry with the distant person and shout at him or her. Many therapists would interpret the distance without betraying (if indeed they felt it) their own wish to be closer. He defines 'ordinary' as 'unexceptional' (Lomas, 1994: 121), but perhaps he is clearer when he contrasts this quality of being ordinary with the impression often conveyed by psychoanalysts that they have some 'mystical' quality about them, that they have become 'qualified masters . . . endowed with a special technique' (Lomas, 1994: 134). The qualities he identifies that make a good therapist are in fact rather special: we might argue that if more people showed them there would be less need of therapists. But these particular qualities are often not taught, or even caught, in the extensive training that therapists undergo, and these qualities do of course appear in 'ordinary' people who have had no training! What are called attributes of a therapist are seen as less vital in traditional trainings than technical and theoretical knowledge; for example, 'wise dealing' is a 'central feature rather than an attribute which has slipped in through the back door' (Lomas, 1981: 14).

What Lomas is perhaps describing above all is an attitude. He uses the term 'the analytic attitude', à la Schafer (1983), in a number of places and Lomas devotes a chapter to this concept in *Cultivating Intuition*. The particular knowledge that a therapist has acquired as a result of life experience, personal therapy and clinical work is expressed in an ordinary way. It is conveyed in the context of a rather ordinary relationship – one that is not mystified by a setting or an attitude that is both confusing to the patient and somewhat grandiose in the therapist. Although Lomas does not quite put it this way, to be ordinary as a therapist is itself something special; and for a therapist to demonstrate the attributes that Lomas identifies is also special for the patient.

Lomas is vexed by the perils of training, which is so often equated with the search for status. He firmly believes in the professional worker, but he stresses that a training group should be non-hierarchical, essentially an enquiry into, and teaching of, the ways in which disturbed people can be helped. He thinks the progression in many people's minds from befriending through counselling and psychotherapy to psychoanalysis is artificial and depends upon 'our caring for status' (Lomas, 1981: 17). Counsellors and therapists, in order to be recognized, have to train with a certain school with its particular technique and theory, and have to keep to 'the straight and narrow' in order to qualify. Yet, as patients are all unique, each person in training is different, and needs something delicate for them as an individual. The rise in Britain of the movement towards registration means that counsellors and therapist try to become 'scientific', although this choice of adjective is not quite correct: 'conformist' might be more accurate. Lomas is himself doubtful of the value of a register, except to exclude people whose moral behaviour falls short of the expected standard. He would, however, make it a requirement that therapists should to give an honest answer when asked about their training and experience.[3]

Lomas has experienced sufficient of one professional group to be wary of psychotherapists and counsellors following suit.

> Psychoanalysts, as a group, have enormous respect for intellectual distinction; they are drawn, by and large, from the socially and professionally elect and usually command a notable erudition: they aim to achieve a respectable place among scientists; the structure of their institutions is hierarchical; they tend to form cliques; and many believe themselves to be in possession of a method (Freud's 'pure gold') which not only surpasses all others but has little to learn from them. (Lomas, 1981: 31)

Although in several places, from his early writing onwards, he refers to societal pressures (e.g. Lomas, 1967a: 24, 138–9; Lomas, 1987b: 100) and believes firmly in the relevance of sociological analysis for therapy, Lomas seldom makes much of what such an analysis can reveal in understanding the dynamics and effects of professionalization. Were he to do so, he might find evidence to support his concern that organizations and professions tend towards rigidity and exclusivity, and demonstrate an inflexibility that can cripple individuality and creativity. His principal criticisms are of psychoanalysis, but some of what he describes is just as true of other types of therapy. He hints at the narrow attitudes in behaviour therapy (Lomas, 1981: 82), the weaknesses in humanistic therapy (Lomas, 1987b: 81), or the mechanical quantification in psychiatry (Lomas, 1973, Ch. 3) but seldom sees that there is the same tendency in these forms of therapy for similar conformity. The pressures that induce the hardening of structures are hard to overcome and it remains to be seen whether the Cambridge training can remain true to its origins. There is no sign of diminishing radicalism in Peter Lomas as he celebrates three-quarters of a century, but will it be possbile to stay the same for those who carry his mantle, under pressure from the normalizing tendency of professional institutions? Effective prophets tend to be found in individuals, and not in groups!

No easy way

The history of psychoanalysis has a number of examples of therapists who have turned their back on analysis in pursuit of more effective methods of working with patients. Sometimes they have claimed success, or promised a less time-consuming or less difficult technique than that which their original training urged upon them. Some have enlarged our discipline with their ideas and ways of practice: others have replaced one set of dogmatically held opinions with another.

Lomas is as distrustful of 'short-cut methods' in therapy as he is of the idealization of charismatic figures. He is suspicious of those who make a break from their particular training background and set up methods that they claim produce sure results, but he never suggests that what he has discovered about therapy is straightforward. Reading his case examples there is no doubt that he always has to watch for the undesirable results of his greater honesty and freedom: such as the patient who idealizes him even more, when Lomas has tried to show the patient that there is no reason to view him as anything other than an fallible human being. He knows that the hazard of wanting to make people happy is also true of himself (Lomas, 1981: 144).

He shares his feelings about therapy with his readers, as much as he will sometimes share his feelings with his patients 'more unreservedly that we usually do' (Lomas, 1981: 142). He certainly does not glamorize. 'It is discomforting to face continued exposure to the hate, confusion, misery, rigidity, or dependence of those whom one must tolerate and even attempt to heal . . . Ultimate failure is particularly hard to bear' (Lomas, 1981: 142–3).

Lomas's work defies cheap jibes or simplistic interpretations. His greatest misgiving about all his writing might be said to echo what is expressed in his first major book: 'the fear that I have conveyed that the spontaneous and open psychotherapeutic approach is easy, or painless' (Lomas, 1973: 150). It is this that makes his departures from traditional technique so convincing.

Notes

1 A remark made on the video In Conversation with Peter Lomas, University of Leicester Audio-Visual Services and Department of Adult Education (1991)
2 All but the last of these virtues appear in The Case for a Personal Psychotherapy (Lomas, 1981: 6–7). 'Intuition' is given special attention in Cultivating Intuition (Lomas, 1994).
3 Much of this paragraph draws upon the brief article, 'Durability of the Talking Cure', Society, November/December 1997, pp. 17–19.

Chapter 2
Interview with Peter Lomas

SIAN MORGAN

SM Peter, I want to begin by asking you about your family of origin.
PL They came from Lancashire. I think of myself as a Celt not an Anglo-Saxon, with bits of Welsh, Scots and Irish. My mother was the daughter of a Congregationalist minister, on the social scale a little bit above my father, who was a Lancashire man with a broad Lancashire accent and I never learnt as much about his background as my mother's, there was quite a lot of drink in the family, which she didn't take to. She was rather proper about these things, as might be expected of the daughter of a minister. He worked his way up from being an office boy to being the managing director of a mill – a cotton mill – and he was very absorbed in his work. He wanted me to follow in his footsteps.
SM Where was the mill?
PL He started in Manchester and then he moved out and got a new mill in Northwich. I had an elder sister, 7 years older. It was quite a gap and I suppose I was, relatively speaking, like an only child. My parents were very loving people but immensely anxious; they worried terribly what the neighbours thought and my mother was very preoccupied with health. My father nearly died of pneumonia when I was three and I think that really shook her and I remember him being looked after as if he was something of an invalid, but of course with Manchester smogs it was difficult to recover from bouts of bronchitis. There was some reason for her concern but I felt very, very sorry for him. Quite a lot of that passed over on to me. I was very much kept away from other children, who were thought to be full of germs. I had quite a lonely childhood until I went to a boys' school when I was 8.
SM You lived in Cheadle Hulme in Cheshire, didn't you?
PL Yes, I liked the school there after I got over the shock of being with

other children. I loved playing football; I played whenever there were daylight hours. I got on well with the other boys. It was a rather crazy school with a very religious, sadistic head teacher. I should say that I had a very religious background.

SM What sort?

PL We were Congregationalists and Non-Conformists. We went to church, but it was the moral atmosphere in the house, with ideas of wickedness and sin. I really feel, when I look back, very claustrophobic.

SM I can sympathize with you,

PL As we moved up the social scale, as my father gradually got more money, we had what was then called a maid who lived in. She was fanatically religious. She indoctrinated me with all sorts of ideas about sin and told me that I would go to the Devil. The most difficult thing for me now, looking back at my childhood, is to understand how my parents permitted me to be so involved with someone whom I quite obviously must have hated. As my father got more money and more ideas, they sent me off to boarding school, to a public school, at 13. I never seemed to have any choice in these matters and I never questioned it. I didn't want to go but I went and was there four years and I hated it. The boys were of a better sort of class than I was and they rather looked down on my accent and my social manners. They were into hunting, shooting and fishing. It wasn't bad educationally but these were not the kind of boys I was used to; they didn't have their warmth and friendliness. They'd been at boarding prep schools. They seemed like a species from another world. I hadn't then got the understanding or confidence to question their values. I hated it but I never asked to be taken away. They had a fagging system, with beatings on bare bottoms and all that kind of rubbish.

SM What happened to your sister?

PL She never escaped the household.

SM So at least it was an escape for you to go away to school . . .

PL It was an escape that didn't work. I had to make my escape later. It was a nasty business; I hurt my parents enormously. I was very angry at their possessiveness. It was one of the worst things in my life and I find it very difficult to bear. My sister spent all her life in the same road. She got married but she never emotionally escaped from them. She didn't suffer from the mental turmoil that I had. She didn't grow up as neurotic in the obvious sense. I suffered from extreme anxiety, which is why I went eventually for psychoanalysis, because I suffered from anxiety attacks.

SM Claustrophobia . . .

PL Claustrophobic feeling; I had not yet got used to the outer world. I had yet to find my way into it. Hence psychoanalysis.

SM But you did a medical training first.
PL My medical training was part of coming from a religious background. I had very strong ideas; my original idea was to become a doctor out in Africa, à la Albert Schweitzer. It didn't come off, because I lost my religious beliefs and I wasn't made for medicine, in a practical way. I was all right on diagnoses and getting on with patients, but not when it came to putting up drips and working in casualty. I hate to think that anyone let me loose to do these things. But I did not feel for a long time that I was in good enough shape to do psychiatry, or psychoanalysis. I worked in general practice for a long time. Then I decided I wanted to train, got a job in London, applied to the Institute, was interviewed by Winnicott who completely captivated me, for at least 10 years! I went to the Institute with great enthusiasm, and was taught by Melanie Klein and many others who were extremely creative – Balint and Marion Milner . . .
SM What excited you most about your training?
PL I think mainly it was a fascination with a way of thinking that was entirely new to me; I was not, in a sense, a well-educated person. I had a vocational training that was awfully narrow; I was fascinated by what made people tick and, for no doubt all sorts of unconscious reasons, I had a desperate desire to be with and to help troubled people, neurotic or psychotic. It was an immensely exciting period. I was working at the Cassel Hospital, which was also a very exciting place, a therapeutic community. It was very avant-garde. Sometimes, looking back, I don't know how much was youthful enthusiasm or how much those times were more exciting than it is now. It certainly was a lot more novel. There certainly was a lot more creativity around. There was a lot more to learn. You know how a discipline at certain stages can be very exciting, while later on it can become a bit ossified. When I was in training there was Winnicott getting up every few weeks and delivering one of these master papers. I always thought he was the best. It took quite a time for him to get accepted. I went off Melanie Klein who had been quite an influence on me.
SM What made you go off her?
PL What made me go off her were the Kleinians themselves and their attitude of omnipotence. I was taught by Paula Heimann and other Kleinians. Their certainty, their arrogance that they knew and the rigidity of their technique and the way of writing, and I began not to believe their ideas. They seemed to me to be a lot of them fantasies.
SM It must have resonated with your religious background.
PL Oh I think so. I've been a little bit of a rebel, since my early twenties.
SM Oh, but I understand your misgivings, the way in which you can feel that you are being taken over by a belief system, which has a fundamentalist quality.

PL It is fundamentalist. It did captivate me for a while. I think one crucial thing in my own analysis occurred when I read a paper which had just come out by colleagues of Gregory Bateson, entitled, 'Pseudo-mutuality in the family relations of schizophrenics' [Wynne *et al.*, 1958] and it approached the subject from an entirely different perspective from the Freudian one. It approached it in terms of confusion, of the confusion of the environment, the falsity of what went on in the family. When I read that, I recognized myself in it. I recognized my own family – not that anyone was schizophrenic. I think a lot has gone wrong with the way in which we think of Gregory Bateson and his work and also that of Ronnie Laing, as if it all hinged on whether their explanation of schizophrenia really is right. God knows, it might all be in the genes, but the phenomenon of confusion is to me instantly recognizable. That started me reading other similar papers and also existentialist writers. I found a paper by Buber which talked in this kind of language. Then I came to meet Ronnie Laing, who was analysed, as I was, by Charles Rycroft. He had a group to which I gave a paper that contained some of these ideas and he was pleased to come across someone else who had been thinking along the same lines. And so I spent quite a lot of time with him and his group and worked with some of the families. He and Esterson wanted me to get involved with a book that they were writing on families and I started to get a bit involved with that, but I soon found that I couldn't work with Ronnie. Ronnie had to be the chief wherever he was; wherever Ronnie was, there was Ronnie and there were disciples.

SM Would you say that your analysis cured you?

PL No. I think it helped me, helped me a lot and I think it educated me.

SM It was a training analysis?

PL I had two. One in Manchester and one in London. Both the people I went to see were better educated than me. They were both flexible enough to talk to me a bit. My first analyst was very rigid but she was a very well-informed person. I can remember very early on saying to her, 'look, I am very uneducated, where the hell do I begin?' She said 'Bernard Shaw' and I think it was the best thing she ever said to me. I fell in love with Bernard Shaw. My analysis did not cure me. I think it took away an absolutely intolerable existential dread. I don't know that it did what Freud said, 'to turn a neurosis into ordinary human misery', but it turned an intolerable dread into ordinary phobic anxiety. Not ordinary, no, because not everyone has it, but a sort of manageable phobic anxiety, which still gets to me when I travel. But I think I have changed at least as much since finishing my analysis as I did before, through working with people, through changing my ideas about life. And of course I felt I had to get away from what I thought was the narrowness of psychoanalysis.

SM Breaking out of another kind of claustrophobia. Breaking out of another kind of possessive environment.
PL Yes, of course, because the Institute is very possessive. Everything was like a religion, very pure and superior. There were the lesser people outside. I couldn't be doing with that.
SM When did you leave the Institute?
PL I suppose between five and 10 years after I had finished training. I didn't leave in any disharmony. I got on with most of the people. I missed them. But I could no longer be comfortable if I called myself a Freudian. However much I valued Freud, I did not feel I could call myself a psychoanalyst.
SM It must have been quite a loss.
PL It was a loss.
SM A loss of stimulus?
PL Yes, a loss of stimulus. A loss of referrals. A loss of status. Nobody ever asked me to speak at analytic meetings. I used to go to international conferences. I can't say it has ever broken my heart. I think I tend to be a bit of a loner. But like most people I am very conflicted. I like being with people. I like talking but I am not much of a social person or a groupie person. I can cope with quite a lot of my own company.
SM The lonely child again.
PL Yes.
SM Shall we stop for a while . . . ?

SM When I was thinking about talking to you, I thought I would like to ask you what you think heals?
PL I don't know that I know but I'll have a go. I can remember writing a review of Marion Milner's book *The Hands of the Living God*, her account of a 20-year analysis with a schizophrenic woman. I wrote it for the *New Statesman*. I wrote quite a bit about it and then I said at the end that I wondered if what really helped this woman was that it must have been obvious to her that Marion Milner loved her. Marion was very touched by that. I thought she would be offended. She had after all written a long volume, illustrated with her patient's pictures, wonderfully thought out and very imaginative. I don't believe that it is as simple as just love, but I do believe that if a patient senses that you care and want them better for non-narcissistic reasons, that that is a very important element in it. I tend to think that what makes people better in therapy is not unlike what makes people better in ordinary life. I am often criticized for using the word 'ordinary', but to me it is central as an idea. Most people seem to need an idea that is central to their work. For most of those working in analytic psychotherapy, Freud's theories are used, such as the idea of transference; others use development as their point of

reference. These ideas are not central to my work though I may use them. What stimulates me, what makes me think and what holds me together is what in the real world would be the ordinary thing to do to help this person. Would it be to try to understand them, would it be to try and talk to them about their childhood, would it be just to sit with them, would it be to put a rocket under them, would it be to hug them? What would be the decent thing to do? I like the word 'decent'. There is someone who has written a book, *The Decent Society* (Margalit, 1996), which I like. I have awful trouble with this idea because it is very difficult to think about it without it seeming as though one is saying that one must be a decent person to be able to do it. I suppose, up to a certain point, I think that is true. I don't think that a psychopath is going to do much good but I don't feel one has to have above-average decency, for the therapist is in a very facilitating position. Someone comes and is saying I want help and, because we are not locked in some terrible emotional predicament with them already, one is given a good chance to be decent. That does not mean that one should not learn whatever one can from Freud, from Winnicott, from the Existentialists, from the Bible, from Tolstoy, from any source that might be useful. But I don't think one should get too far from what I think of as ordinariness. If I find myself being stilted professionally, I think, "Stop it!". I think the same about writing about therapy. It should be done in ordinary language. I think specialized language can get between us. In the end I think what heals is a bit of a mystery.

SM I think that unfortunately over the last 15-or-so years, the language of psychoanalysis has been appropriated by academics. That the idea of healing has got lost and that understanding for its own sake has become too central to the endeavour.

PL Even the word 'healing' is suspect. It is thought to be mushy and not scientific enough. I think it is comparable to what has happened in the study of literature. At one time one could read great literary critics, even as recently as Leavis, and it was written in ordinary language. But if you read a post-structuralist on a poem, any ordinary relationship to the poem is lost. It is as if many people have become terrified of having a natural response to a poem or a painting in case they are torn apart by the deconstructionists. It is a parallel with what I think has happened in the world of psychotherapy,

SM My impression is that it becomes quite a sterile discourse.

PL Yes. I think another thing is that the therapist is in quite a vulnerable position. So, of course, is the patient. So there are two quite vulnerable people, both pushing up defences and the therapist has a hard job and needs to look after him or herself and tends to adopt distancing techniques. I think therapists are very afraid of being revealed as ordinary human beings who can be petty, stupid, silly, nasty and who don't want to be revealed as they really are. How on earth can you write about what goes on between two people in a consulting room without revealing what the therapist is really like? I think the truth comes from both sides. There are therapists all over the place who think and do things that don't get into the books. Even when one is apparently being candid there are subtle ways of defending oneself. There is a big problem about communicating what goes on.

SM While you were talking I was thinking about the problem of remembering what went on in my own therapy, my experience of being in therapy with you. I am very struck by one of the few things I do remember, which was something which, if you are analytically trained, breaks the rules. It was a self-disclosure. After I had told you how anxious I was about going out, you said that you had actually experienced similar anxiety yourself. I felt such relief, such enormous relief, that although I have felt some anxiety since then, it has been nothing of similar proportion. I no longer felt that I was the only person in the world to have experienced such anxiety. I had always known rationally that I was not the only person to suffer such anxiety but no matter how well I knew that, it never had the same impact on me as your telling me that you had some personal knowledge of the solitary anguish I had experienced.

PL It is funny that it should take a disclosure in a therapeutic setting to have that effect. There is some sort of real relationship, the sort of relationship that does not readily occur elsewhere. I think if things are going well in the therapy, then things carry more conviction and one knows that the therapist is not saying whatever they are saying to make you feel better. I think you knew me well enough to know that I was telling you the truth. What you have just said does take me back to what we were talking about, the difficulty of reporting on what goes on in therapy. It seems to me we could have gone through this interview without it being mentioned that you had been in therapy with me. It is a real fact between us which presumably you do not mind revealing, but which so often goes unsaid. It is a significant aspect of this interview and people will make of it what they like.

SM They certainly will; probably concluding that the whole enterprise is dubious because it involves a transgression of boundaries and is indeed thoroughly incestuous! On the contrary, part of the reason that I think what you said to me helped was that you were continually challenging my need to be treated as a special case, which I think eventually got through to me, but it did take a long time.

PL Yes, I think there can be a confusion about going back to one's development. It can be very important to take one's development into account but that is very different from thinking about it as being special in a way that gives one a right to feel that one has a grievance; that one has a harder time than other people. I don't know how one measures hard times and obviously some people have far harder times than others. Some children do have a very hard time. But once the patient in therapy thinks they have had an unduly bad deal and that can account for how they are and that they had no part in it and have now no part in it, then it is finished. [Laughter] You see we laughed. Laughter is the sort of thing that isn't reported when therapists write about their work. Humour and fun can help to take away dread.

SM We often talk about creativity but I think we might underestimate the value of frivolity, especially those of us who come from puritanical cultures. I don't mean that we should be manic but I mean that we should feel that we can share pleasure in things that are meaningless and thereby finding ways of not attaching too much significance to things and to ourselves.

PL There is an awful danger in analysis of over-analysing. It can kill the relationship. It is like a child playing and being watched. It creates a heaviness and there can be so much heaviness in psychotherapeutic meetings and discussions. It may be because people feel that they are being watched, but there may be more to it than that. There is, I think, sometimes a kind of seriousness which is not unlike the kind of seriousness that can occur in some types of religious groups, where one is not allowed to say 'fuck'.

SM A solemnity.

SM You are very obviously interested in the training of psychotherapists and have been part of a group which has set up a training in Cambridge. Could you talk to me about how you feel a person should train to be a therapist?

PL Yes, I suppose my philosophy of training follows from the idea that it is an ordinary pursuit and less of a specialized pursuit than one would think, and that it is not simply a question of learning techniques. What originally stirred me was that when I trained, it was mainly specialized people who were being trained; it was a great advantage to be a doctor. It was an advantage to have a degree, particularly a relevant degree. It probably is still to some extent. It was a great advantage to be an intellectual. It seemed to me that it was not always people with this kind of background who were necessarily best suited to help those in distress. Some people who were naturally gifted and very intuitive were not being taken in by the Freudian Institute. It seemed to me that one needed a place where one could extend training to those who did not come from an 'appropriate' background. It seems to me that there is no reason why a bus-driver should not walk into the Freudian Institute and be trained as an analyst, if he were gifted. It was this kind of thinking that led me to consider setting up a training that was later to become the Guild of Psychotherapists. More and more, as time has gone by, I have thought that the usual way of training is not satisfactory, in that it does not give enough weight to the general way a person behaves and thinks and feels towards someone who is distressed; to the experience of being with people and of getting as much help as is possible from colleagues and supervisors. There is too much stress placed on working with particular techniques. I think that one of the absurd characteristics of the current psychotherapeutic scene is that it consists of a multiplicity of techniques; it is a veritable Tower of Babel. It is as if one chooses a technique out of a basket and that there is now a certified body, the UKCP, who will say, 'Oh you've got this technique, all we want to know is whether you've learnt it well. and whether someone else will vouch for you. If that's the case we'll have you.' I think therapy is very much a personal affair. It is not wise to try to make clones of people by making them Freudians or whatever. Student therapists have to find their own way of being with people that will help them. One can expose them to all sorts of marvellous people such as Ferenczi (who is one of my heroes), and it will do them a lot of good, but that is not the business. The business is to do with finding their own way, using their own intuition, learning to be themselves in the presence of someone who is asking for help, who is probably putting all kinds of pressures on them. I am quite orthodox in the sense that I believe that people who train should themselves have experience of being in therapy, to learn about themselves and to learn how to cope when they are put under pressure. To give this kind of individual training is very difficult in this present climate of opinion and is becoming progressively more difficult, because those who want registration, in order to be able to say to the public, these people are 'OK' and only these people are 'OK', need to do it as neatly and scientifically and rationally and quantifiably as possible. What is forgotten in this: that we who want to teach, want to help a trainee therapist to be in a room with someone in distress. We should not be requiring them to be theoreticians (though it would be very good if more people could enlarge the scope of our knowledge), but that is not what training is about. We need to know if a trainee is safe to be left in a room with someone who is distressed. A very unpopular view.

SM You have recently written a book about the limitations of technique in psychotherapy?

PL Yes, that's right. I have actually called it *How Should One Live?* – which is a very broad title, the subtitle is 'The Limitations of Technique in Psychotherapy'. The reason I wanted to write the book is because I have come increasingly to think that everything that goes on within psychotherapy does bring up the question as to what is a good way of living and what is a bad way of living. Even if one makes an interpretation that is supposed to be neutral, an analyst selects an interpretation on the basis of their moral stance. If they think there is something dodgy about what their patient is doing, their interpretation will not only reflect their technique but their moral view, and beyond that, on how they think a decent person should live. On some occasions the issues will be ones that most people will probably agree upon. I would imagine that most people would agree that it is not a good idea to go round telling lies all the time or, to take it to an extreme, to abuse children. But for most of the time the issues that come up are likely to be issues over which there are likely to be quite a difference of opinion between therapists. To take another example, should one always remain sexually faithful in marriage? Interpretations that could be made might involve ideas derived from Freud on the Oedipus Complex, ideas involving things to do with dependence and independence. If you behave this way it shows you are too dependent on your wife. It shows you can't have a flirtation because you have a mother fixation. On the other hand, if you show a tendency towards being flirtatious, you are promiscuous and you have never been able to settle for a loved object. You have always denied your dependence on your mother. If you read the literature these underlying moral attitudes are completely ignored. It is all a matter of technique based upon a theory. A therapist is not concerned with morals according to that view. It would be awful to be caught moralizing. It might even be thought of as a religion. Another way I think morals comes into the work is to do with the way one behaves with the person, because if one adopts a strict technique one is saying to the patient, 'this is the way we are going to do this: you lie on the couch; you can ask me as many questions as you like but I am not going to answer them.' The whole set-up of the communication is ordained by the therapist and the therapist will defend it by saying this is the right technique and it works. If you do this then you will get better, which is quite a logical argument if one were absolutely sure that this was the right thing to do and that it were as sure as a dose of penicillin in a case of pneumonia.

SM Whereas what might be happening might be that the patient was responding positively to suggestion: The suggestion 'If you lie on the couch I will not engage with you directly, and implicitly you will get better'.

PL Yes, the patient might well get better because the magic potion has been given. The other way of looking at it is to look at it morally: is it morally right that in an engagement between two people, that it should be set up so that one person is so dominant; that the therapist is the one who makes the rules? How undermining is it for the patient for this to be the case? Now if you take it out of the therapeutic setting and you see two people talking together and one is making all the rules, one would probably say that that was bullying and that it was not morally right. The more one gets away in therapy from ordinary human decency, with respect for the other person, the more that one should look to see if one is justified. One can justify all kinds of behaviour; there are people who can justify going to bed with every patient who comes to see them; there are people who can justify using all kinds of methods of eliciting so-called repressed memories of abuse and may put their patients in hospital and use drugs to elicit these so-called repressed memories. How much harm does that do, in the name of technique? The only morality that would come into it would be if one said that the technique could be justified, on a moral basis. But using any ordinary standards of behaviour, it stinks.

SM Where do you then derive your own decent, ordinary standards of behaviour from?

PL Well, that is why this book has a question mark at the end! *How Should we Live?* I can't imply that I know how to live any more than the next person, any more than my patient, because I don't. I can only fall back, as we do in any situation in life, on what I feel is decent behaviour. In his lovely book *The Decent Society*, Margalit says that decency is more important than equality, however important equality is.

SM It is respect for the other person.

PL It's very close to respect. If you give respect to the other person, as best you can, then I do not think you are likely to go far wrong.

SM What about the possibly deceptive nature of consciousness, if you believe in unconscious process?

PL Yes, I don't think that that alters the argument, it just complicates it. It is absolutely central to me in therapy to make things conscious that have been denied. But I think there is a danger in psychotherapy to be so absolutely focused on that, so that others things are forgotten, I think it was a terrifically important discovery. It wasn't really a discovery because people had thought of it before Freud. But it was a terrifically important insight, as one way in which people can be helped out of confusion, out of mess, is this focus on what they are denying and on the various defences that they can use to keep things out of consciousness. Important though that is, however, I don't think that that aim should skew the relationship. Of the many problems that consciousness or unconsciousness brings, there is one to me that is the most difficult and that is to know when a person is responsible for their actions, because the whole question of unconscious aims then comes into the debate and then I think one has to fall back largely on one's intuition, as to whether or not a person can help what they are doing. For example, if someone says, 'Look, I can't go out of the house because I am too afraid', and gets people to accommodate to that, I sometimes think it is very difficult to be sure. I think one could interpret it, and it can be very useful to explore what it might be about. It might be helpful to explore why they have such an unreasonable anxiety. It might be because they were afraid of being looked at in the street and of being thought of as homosexual or mad or whatever, and it could be very useful to explore the various possible interpretations. But I think one could look at it in a totally different way and say 'Isn't it about time you tried? You have all these people being put to inconvenience, who have to do your shopping for you. Isn't it about time you were less selfish?' This is a moral thing to say to somebody and I do occasionally say this sort of thing, but I do feel uncomfortable. Not because it is not the sort of thing a psychoanalyst is supposed to say, because I've long ago stopped worrying about that. But I worry whether it is moralizing, either in the sense of implying that one knows how to behave or whether it is a misjudgement of just how disabled the person really is. It might be no better than someone coming in for the first time to a therapeutic session saying , 'I feel so anxious, I am shaking all over', and for one to tell them to pull themselves together. So I feel a bit uneasy that I might be doing something as crude as that. However, one usually knows the person pretty well by the time one is likely to say something like that. And one might be right or wrong. It does bring up the question as to whether a therapist has a right to say to a person, 'I think you should do this' or 'I think you should do that.'

SM -Can I just interject here, because I remember that you said something of this kind to me once. When I was feeling phobic after Catherine was born, I phoned you up to tell you I was feeling frightened and that I didn't feel I could leave the house, and you said 'I think you should come'. It was one of the many boundaries you set for me, which helped contain me. I think if you had said, 'Oh, leave it for today then, or I'll come to see you' then I think I would have remained in a stuck regression. I remember it was uncomfortable but no more than uncomfortable. Your attitude made me feel that you had faith that I would not fall apart.

PL I remember now. It's funny that I have been saying all this and that I had forgotten it applied to you. It was at the beginning of the therapy and I had quite a tussle with myself as to whether I had the right to say it and it came from the guts. I think it might have conveyed to you, too, that I cared whether you came or not.

SM Yes, I think it did. I think it was a very important boundary and marker that you were real and not just a product of my fantasy or a product of what was going on in my mind at the time, because I had collapsed in on myself. These are boundaries that it is necessary to define from time to time. You are talking about the need to put boundaries on behaviour, aren't you?

PL Ye-es. In what way are these boundaries . . . ?

SM They are moral boundaries, because you are saying 'I will help you but you've got to meet me somewhere along the line between us'.

PL Yes. I am not omnipotent. I have my limitations. I have said something like that to a person when I felt rather desperate with someone who had got stuck and was in a bad way. I can't remember how I worded it but it was almost an appeal. It sounds rather awful to say it, but it was something like 'look, if you won't do it for yourself, what about me?' It seems to go against the theory of allowing the patient to express their true self and not to impose a super-ego morality upon them to which they might adapt. But I think it is a question of what seems appropriate no matter what the theories are.

SM It is not a harsh super-ego morality . . .

PL It is not speaking from above; I don't know whether it is speaking from below.

SM Leading on from what you are talking about, to do with issues of responsibility, I'd like to ask you what you think about regression as a technique as opposed to what happens to people spontaneously when in therapy.

PL I think you've hit on another subject that I find intellectually very difficult because I have been very influenced by Winnicott. I have known people go through regression to what he would call the 'true self', which does seem to have been very rewarding. On the other hand, when that has happened it does seem to have been very muddled; there is this division which Balint makes, isn't there, between benign and malignant regression? To me, if someone collapses and falls apart there is usually a horrid mixture and I think that the result that comes out is not usually some beautiful new self. But I do think that in the collapse from being a functioning adult self and the withdrawal into being somebody rather helpless, there is the potential for new growth and it has very often seemed that growth can occur. I think occasionally that can be illusory, in the same way that going away on holiday and feeling very much better can be illusory, in that it does not necessarily mean that one has come back a changed person but one has come back a refreshed person. One needed the holiday very much indeed. In the same way a person can need a regression very much no matter what form it takes. It can take the form of illness, of a holiday, or it can take the form of a regression in therapy. It does not necessarily mean it will take on the creative form that Winnicott describes. The word is a bit of a problem too, because it implies a going back to childhood experience and I'm not convinced that that is always a major feature in it. The major feature to me seems to be the collapse of defences which occurs, so that the person in the present is in a state that is akin to the state of a helpless child and is very dependent on those around him. I do not think that it necessarily involves going back to what Freud called a fixation point in time when something crucial happened, which is how Winnicott sees it. I think that can happen, but in most cases what I think happens is that there is a collapse of defences which may be major but can also be quite minor. One does not usually think of crying as a regression, but I have almost prayed sometimes that certain patients would cry. I'd give anything for them to let themselves collapse, to feel their despair. That is not what is usually called regression but to me it is the same kind of phenomenon. It does bring up a moral question as to how much this, when it happens, is authentic. Are the tears real tears, are they hysterical, are they manipulative? I think there are people who can read books about regression, as people do, and construct a regression to fit the theory. Again, I think that one is left with one's intuition as to whether one is confronted with someone who is making greedy or omnipotent demands to be looked after, that accentuates their weakness and incapacity, in the sort of way Thomas Szasz talks about in *The Myth of Mental Illness*. (Szasz, 1961). Or whether it is something that has come upon them by accident, sometimes a real accident, and which they are risking, trusting letting themselves be helpless and dependent. Something that a good therapist might intuitively accept and respect. Once again there are no rules in this, no technique . . .

SM Just your senses and your intuition . . .

PL Just as a parent might be with a child who won't go to school.

SM Do you think there is a particular risk for psychotherapists and psychoanalysts that they might become narcissistic, if they are not already?

PL Yes I do. I don't think that people who decide to train as psychotherapists are necessarily more narcissistic than other people. But I think they might easily be tempted to grow into narcissists. the temptations really are rather awful. One is put in a position of someone who is so wise that they can actually help another human being to live better. It is quite different from the expertise of say someone who is an electrician, who has got it all at his finger-tips as to which wires go where, but we don't think of him as a god-like person coming in. Whereas in therapy it is very different; a person comes to see you who is lost and wants a saviour and one can very easily come to believe that that is what one is. The language presents a temptation because the language describes a theory about living. Freud's theory implies that one has a better grasp of what living is about. Of course we don't. Even the fact of having a special language is itself a temptation to narcissism because it is the language of someone elevated in a hierarchy, like a priest's use of Latin. But I think there is another way in which a therapist can become defensively narcissistic. I am thinking about narcissism in a slightly different way, not as feeling god-like but in falling back on a particular role which is used defensively; they are not being ordinary. The therapist has a special way of conducting himself. It might be that he sits back in his chair and grunts. I think one can get rather complacent that one knows how to handle oneself. Mind you, I sometimes think that the only place in the world that I can handle myself properly is in my consulting room. Once I go out of it I am lost! I think therapists often put on all sorts of voices. One can develop a therapeutic voice, which carries implications of subtleness, of shrewdness, of wisdom – I am sitting back, I have seen everything, heard everything. You know how a priest can have a special voice, that you can spot in a moment. Psychotherapists can have a similar voice, particularly in groups. I know I am going a bit deaf, but I find psychotherapists in groups more difficult to hear than most people. They have most of them got a rather soothing, quiet voice. One plays a role all one's life. There is no such thing in a sense as being ordinary, because one is always doing something. If I go home, I play the role of husband, but I hope that it drops off me so that I feel differently from how I felt when I went up to the altar. But one can also hang on to these rigidities. One's patients, it seems to me, so intensely want us to be real and sometimes, when I have been real with a person they have been so moved, tears have come into their eyes. I know it cannot be justified theoretically, it might not be a clever or particularly wise communication, but it feels as if it has really meant something to my patient, and that it was a good thing. It feels as if it is the result of having disengaged myself from the role of being the therapist.

SM Sometimes it can be something as simple as conveying to someone that you like them.

PL Yes, and they will know whether you mean it. Or it might be something rather indirect that conveys that. It is quite surprising that one can be someone's therapist for a long time and work awfully hard and care for them and then suddenly one does something different or out of context. It might be to say 'you don't look well, perhaps you should go and see your doctor', or 'you look tired, perhaps you should go to bed early', something that you say spontaneously that makes the person think that 'this isn't a game – she means it'.

SM Why do you think therapists do need their theory so badly?

PL I think one thing is that people like to have a creed, a belief system. Some kind of system that makes us think we know what's going on, whereas in actual fact I don't think we know why the hell we are here or what is going on. I think psychotherapists need theory to justify what they are doing. In the private sector someone comes and pays money and therapists need to feel they are giving something back. I think many people in other professions have that kind of feeling. I think a doctor has that kind of feeling. I remember when I worked as a GP feeling that I must give them something, and I was very tempted to give them pills to make them feel their visit had been worth while. I used to give them tonics or cough mixtures which were nice and pink and tasted nasty. We can't give tonics but if we can give an expert theory, a really good, deep interpretation, then we feel we have done something. It is not very comfortable to feel that one has not much more to fall back on than whatever intelligence, decency, wisdom, and sensitivity that one happens to possess, and that may or may not be of a high calibre. Basically that is primarily what we have got. I think we can be helped a lot by what we learn about in our training, the big thing being the unveiling of what we are not aware of. I don't think the concept of the unconscious is difficult, but one can make it very difficult to understand. To know that people hide things from themselves is very simple.

SM Is there anything else that you particularly value in theory?

PL Transference. Again, not necessarily as it is thought of by analysts, that what happens is a repetition either of a reality or a fantasy of what went on with, say, a particular parent (though of course that can happen) but it can be more that the child, largely through the influence of the family, comes to think about the world in certain ways based on his or her experience. The child grows up to become an adult and those old patterns of thought persist and sometimes become rigid and are no longer appropriate to the present day, and so they are not seeing the present day reality. The present becomes distorted. If, for example, they have been spoilt, they expect to be spoilt and will expect that in therapy. In fact will be more obviously there, because they have come in order to reveal themselves. They are trying to be more open because what's going on can be looked at. If the patient persistently comes up with certain expectations or fantasies about the therapist which are not true then the therapist will be able to say 'Why do you persistently think x when it is not the case? You have always assumed from the very beginning that I am not married, just because there is no-one else in the building but I am in fact married.' That is a very simple example but, of course, it can be very subtle. It is something that is part of ordinary life but it has never been taken notice of with anything like the degree of intensity that psychoanalysis dealt with it. I do value the ideas of the unconscious and of transference that psychoanalysis has given us, but what I think is so wrong is the way in which psychoanalysts interpret everything in terms of transference. For one thing it is not true and for another it is bewildering for patients. It undermines their perceptions, with the consequence that I sometimes think that the concept of transference in practice has become more of a disadvantage than an advantage. People can be nearly driven mad by transference interpretations – perhaps they *have* been driven mad. I think another thing that makes therapists want to have a theory is what seems to be almost a terror of being thought naïve and not shrewd enough. I don't know why this should pose such a threat but therapists seem very afraid of being thought simple-minded. That is rather similar to academe; if one can construct a complicated theory then one is thought to be clever, even if one is wrong!

SM People place great value on abstract structures.

PL That's right, they are idealized and it does require great dedication to read these books to understand these theories. That is an achievement that can be seen, even if the person gets it wrong, The terror which students speak of, of saying something and someone then saying 'haven't you read such and such a book'. One is never free of it. I am certainly not; if I write something, someone might then review it and say, 'if you had read Lacan . . . '

SM Can I just ask you what you do think of Lacan?

PL Lacan is not one of my favourite boys. I value clarity very much. Clarity is ordinary. It is concerned with decency, with respect, with avoiding confusion; the undermining of many people is the consequence of a lack of clarity and of confusion. Lacan seems to me to be almost gleeful in his attempts to be gnomic. I do not think he respects his readers. I would not go as a patient to such an arrogant man. I have read some Lacan and I have read several books about Lacan, but because I do not like the way he writes, I have not extensively read what he has written. In so far as I understand his theories I think he is wrong. I do not think that children are as unintegrated as he maintains; of course, they are not whole. I think this is quite a good example of what I was describing, of people being afraid to be naïve. It is considered to be an accolade for a therapist to be someone who can be seen to understand Lacan. I don't want to finish on that negative note.

SM Peter, who do you like and who do you draw your inspiration from?

PL I'm in great danger here of sounding banal, when I say I draw inspiration from patients. It is a bit like writing a book and saying I draw all my inspiration from my wife. It might well be true but it is almost a convention. But I have learnt a hell of a lot from my patients and I draw inspiration from them as people. They do also sometimes drive me mad. And of course I draw inspiration from ordinary people in ordinary life, colleagues, friends. In particular I have been having a correspondence with my colleague Ben Churchill for the last 30 years, with an emphasis on the subject of morality, which has had a definite influence on me. I have also discussed my work over many years with my wife, Diana, who has also deeply influenced my thinking. But perhaps you are also thinking of people in the trade and there are a lot. I want to mention Ferenczi; he was a bit wild (all heroes are) but he was so courageous, in spite of his devotion to Freud. He could take such risks; I so admire the things he did with his patients. I remember Winnicott saying (Winnicott of all people!) 'I sometimes despair of having a new thought, without finding out that Freud had already thought it.' I sometimes think that about Ferenczi. Here am I more than 50 years later writing stuff that I've thought out, and after labouring and labouring, might feel quite pleased with it and I'll go and look up my *Clinical Diary* of Ferenczi and I find that if he hadn't said quite the same thing, then he had already thought something very similar, which is sort of encouraging but sort of puts me in my place a bit. I need hardly mention Freud. Freud does not appeal to me as a person but he did write beautifully. Ferenczi is the person who leads me away from the narrowness of psychoanalysis, towards being what I feel is more myself, more ordinary. Ferenczi was more ordinary. I was inspired too by Winnicott, who taught and supervised me and whom I got to know, along with his wife. He had probably more influence on me than anyone else. Latterly I have become more critical of his emphasis on being able to go back in detail to very early life. I do not like the way he manages to convey that he can do it better. His narcissism can be quite undermining. I find something a little bit precious in Winnicott that wasn't there in Ferenczi. But I have no doubt he is a major figure. There are people outside the analytic tradition who are neglected. The one that most comes to mind is Ian Suttie. He had all the ideas of the Object Relations School and put them in better English, but you don't find mention of him in the analytic books. He is neglected. [See Suttie, 1935.] There is Paul Halmos's book *The Faith of the Counsellors* (Halmos, 1965): another much-neglected book. I was inspired by the American writers on the families of schizophrenics; they gave to me a new dimension, the dimension of family dynamics.

SM   And Harold Searles?

PL   I do admire Harold Searles greatly. I do so admire the doggedness of his work. His writings have been an inspiration; they are in the analytic tradition and sometimes I do not like the language, but some of his papers have made a deep impression on me: 'Oedipal Love in the Countertransference' (Searles, 1959b), a paper about the importance to the child of the parents' appreciation of their emerging sexuality, a very daring paper, a beautiful paper. And in his book on countertransference, his emphasis on the schizophrenic's need to cure not only their parent but also to cure the analyst (Searles, 1979). And the paper 'On the Effort to Drive the Other Person Crazy' (Searles, 1959a).

SM He is a very honest writer.

PL That's right, he is honest, he does not hide, he shows his vulnerability. Also he has the ability to say something striking, which may not be quite true but one remembers it. For example when he says there are certain patients who in order for them to get better, you have to be the most important person in their life. That is a very brave thing to say.

SM I think we may have come to the end of the interview. Before we finish I'd like to thank you for talking to me and also for the help and inspiration you have provided for so many people. I would like to say just one more thing; that there are times, and I almost hesitate to say this, that I feel you might be quite an extraordinary man!

Chapter 3
Peter Lomas: therapy and 'the Outfit'

CAROL DASGUPTA

There was no one there.

Understandably nervous about entering into a therapy in any case, I became increasingly doubtful as I stood in front of the unresponsive door. Had I mistaken the time of the first appointment? Had he forgotten me? (This, to my mind, seemed the likeliest explanation.) Was he using some ghastly test on me? Why was I beginning to feel so angry and, most surprising of all, rather tearful?

In the course of the next six years, both in therapy with Peter and as a student in 'the Outfit', I began to understand what that incident had meant to me and why it had had so profound an effect. An ordinary, real life occurrence (Peter had had to leave Cambridge suddenly to visit a sick relative) provided an unexpected focus for exploring significant personal issues as they emerged during the therapy. Of course, as anyone who knows Peter will realize, insight, acceptance and understanding came about gradually within an atmosphere of calm, unhurried tolerance and what felt like a genuine attempt to understand; punctuated occasionally with surprising and unexpected confrontations.

I had met Peter once before. I had come to a point in life when at last I felt able to indulge in a long-desired therapy. At the time it seemed important for me to seek out and get the therapist who was the 'best', the 'most important', the 'most famous', and it almost goes without saying, male. My search for exactly the right person with whom to work through my transference issues was being undertaken, as the daughter of a successful and important man, blindly, with absolutely no insight as to what I was doing. Peter seemed to have all the necessary attributes, but I was surprised, shocked, perhaps a little disappointed, that he looked so ordinary as he opened the door to me for our first assessment meeting. His clothes were ordinary, his furniture, pictures, and ornaments looked ordinary, as was his manner and conversation. This was far removed from fantasies I must have entertained, that this therapy business was to be fantastic and extraordinary. It was only during the course of my therapy, and as a student reading Peter's books in which the word 'ordinary' assumes special meaning, that I became able to recognize and accept the power, strength, and freeing quality of the ordinary, as opposed to the extraordinary, in living a life.

The front door was to assume a significance that seems hard to explain. It has been opened to me two or three times a week for the last six years. And yet it has remained a surprisingly hard barrier to negotiate. We greet each other formally – no expression of relief, joy, longing, fear, anxiety – just a necessary mechanical manoeuvre to get to the next stage, sitting or lying down in the ordinary room. I know that I wanted a lot more than that – ideally a sign that he was pleased to see me, that I was somehow 'special'. That was what I wanted, but my rational side told me that he was just doing a job. It was well into the therapy before we managed to start talking about this. After all, talking to someone in depth about what it is like to walk through an opened front door seems by everyday, normal standards to be a strange thing, suggestive perhaps of an intimacy and a vulnerability that may be awkward to think or talk about. Ultimately, and after more than a few false starts that had involved a little bit of confrontation and a lot of me squirming around at Peter's tenacity, we were able to engage in a most intimate conversation: about what it felt like to be so distant with each other; who it was, of the two of us, who needed to keep it all so formal; about the risks and anxieties, on my part, involved in a less distant, more open, greeting on the threshold. Not very deep material involving complicated analysis; just a conversation, albeit an intense and difficult one, about a very ordinary, everyday situation. But it was a conversation that enabled a most remarkable loosening up of that particular relationship, and other more general relationships.

In any therapy, the issue of dependency must be one of the most crucial concerns. Peter sat silently during many sessions when we discussed breaks or absences, and I would quite happily and confidently tell him how useful I would find the spare time; on one occasion I told him how relieved I was that we would miss the next session, for I really needed to go to Sainsburys. 'Going to Sainsburys' later became typical of the kind of catchphrase that can express so much in an intimate relationship. Here, we both knew it referred to the common understanding we had achieved about my long-standing difficulty, in and out of therapy, of allowing myself to experience dependence, trust and openness. He sat with me for more than two years while I continued to deny any of his suggestions that maybe I would miss our sessions, or that the breaks might be at all hard for me. Peter let me be as slow as I needed in my understanding of this, tolerating angry accusations of being bored, of going to sleep, of preferring sessions with others. Looking back, I realize that his offer of both patience and gentle firmness provided the facilitating environment that allows a person to develop in their own time, taking risks within the safety of being firmly held. It allowed me to face painful, unrecognized but strangely familiar feelings of rejection, insignificance and inadequacy. No wonder I needed to maintain my 'poise' so carefully; and 'poise' became another catchphrase that crept into our joint vocabulary, not only as a shorthand expression for something complicated and difficult for me to understand, but also as a word that was used teasingly and playfully. Increasingly, as my poise diminished and I started to enjoy a more spontaneous relationship, words and phrases became our playthings, batted back and forth, and we had fun as we played together.

This is not to imply that all sessions were easy or comfortable. The following vignettes perhaps give some idea of how difficult issues were addressed in the therapy. About three years into my therapy, Peter went down with a bad bout of 'flu that lasted about three weeks. This was probably the first time that I experienced, intensely and painfully, the extent of my dependence on him. Not only did I long to resume our sessions – I also became increasingly anxious that he might never work again, or that he might even die. It was when he returned to work that I was able to talk about my fears for him and how important he was to me. While it seemed that this declaration was inevitable, nothing before this examination of our relationship had reached to such limits of intimacy, or had felt so difficult.

Earlier on in the therapy, Peter and I had a fairly minor argument about a bill, Peter claiming that I owed him for a missed session while I had assumed that I did not. Our conversation, mundane and down-to-earth and non-confrontational, opened my eyes to the most uncomfortable realization that, at least on this issue but probably on a much wider level, I could be, without knowing it, rather selfish.

Talking to Peter was never like talking to a blank screen. He was engaged in the dialogue: sometimes as a listener, sometimes more actively. His engagement was perhaps the feature that made our sessions so productive. For there was no hiding behind anything: we were both exposed to each other. Peter's emotions became more evident to me. I saw from his eyes how greatly he missed the company of an old and beloved friend who now lived far away. I realized that he found the experience of ageing unpleasant and disagreeable. I suppose I trusted that he knew enough about, or at least recognized, his own emotions for it to feel safe for me to explore my own. But there are areas, most notably my own worries about growing older, that I have probably not explored in much depth, suggesting a concern with Peter's well-being.

For some time I felt bound by the constraints of the 'rules' of therapy. I did not have a very clear idea of what exactly they were, but technical terms were frequently in my mind and I was sometimes puzzled, probably a bit disappointed, that our sessions were so jargon and theory-free. I wondered if I was getting value for money. One day I started talking to Peter about the Matisse poster in his room, although I don't think I considered the conversation to be 'proper therapy'. I realized in the course of this conversation that Peter and I shared a passion for Matisse, and over the next few sessions we talked of our shared fantasies of flying to New York to see the large Matisse exhibition. An ordinary conversation had become therapy without me knowing it, and this happened over and over again. These everyday conversations often seemed to get to the heart of things, but there were difficulties. For example, I had asked Peter one day something about the Outfit, and became increasingly irritated at the length of his unnecessarily detailed reply. The friendly nature of that conversation probably inhibited me from voicing the frustration I felt, and so precluded the possibility of more conventional therapeutic work.

Sometimes Peter would communicate his countertransferences to me and these, not surprisingly, usually confronted me with aspects of myself I didn't like or even want to know about. On one occasion he warned me that he might receive an important telephone call during the session, and in fact the call did come and he did answer it. After we resumed the session, it became evident that I was feeling angry at the interruption to my time. Peter told me that he had felt it necessary to warn me (though not his other patients that day) about the possibility of the interruption because he was so strongly aware of my propensity to feel anger at any suggestion that I was not being taken seriously enough. I was shocked and upset to hear this (I like to think of myself as fairly easy going) but the episode helped me yet again confront deep-seated feelings of hurt and rejection.

Hearing Peter use the words 'my countertransference to you' on this occasion is just one small example of the enormous contribution my own therapy has had on my learning to be a psychotherapist, and there is no doubt in my mind that therapy has been the single most important element of my training. By talking about what was really going on in the room, I learned more about psychoanalytic concepts such as transference and countertransference, the unconscious, narcissism and envy, than any book has offered. It is also my own therapy that has taught me about <u>being</u> a therapist: about consistency and continuity; about expressing ordinary concerns and comments on life; about the expression of humour; about when to give something away and when to remain obdurate. I also learned to trust in the power of the unorthodox (within the safety and security of a good therapeutic relationship). One particular issue kept resurfacing in sessions over the years, even though it had apparently been worked through. One day I moaned in exasperation 'Why can't I let it go? What else must I do?' Peter's response, 'just stop it' – startlingly non-analytical (though coming after years of more conventional responses) – seems to have worked for I am now much freer from that particular bug.

* * * * *

I applied to join the Outfit as a student one-and-a-half years after I had started therapy with Peter. We talked a great deal about this: why I wanted to become a psychotherapist; why this kind of training; what it might be like for me to be in therapy with someone who was not only deeply involved with the Outfit but had also been the original driving force.

I had first heard about the Outfit in a large garden on a hot summer evening. I was, at the time, training as a counsellor in California and was somewhat in love with this new way of looking at people and the world – it represented the beginning of freedom from an existence that was too tight, rigid and restrained for me. I was terribly keen to continue to train as a psychotherapist, but the prospect of that looked bleak to me. The psychotherapy trainings I had investigated (all of them in London) seemed to replicate, in various manifestations, all the attributes of a past that I was trying to change. It seemed like a dream come true to be hearing about the Outfit's training: students taking responsibility for creating their own training, determining what they want and how to obtain it; contributing what they can to the student group and asking from it, and from the trained members, what they need; the absence of hierarchies and authority and the respect offered to each individual. As it turned out, my training in the Outfit was to be a rich and rewarding experience, which gave me as much opportunity for personal growth as my therapy. But it was not without difficulties.

The idea of joining the Outfit as a student was for me, and I imagine for others, an exciting prospect. The selection procedure, though rigorous and demanding, never seemed to me to be too formidable or anxiety provoking. The procedure was clearly described in the written information sent to me after my initial enquiry about training. A meeting was set up with a student member and this relaxed first contact provided a good environment for me to ask questions freely, without the kind of inhibitions inherent in a more formal setting. I think I got a good sense of how the student group worked in terms of its structure and academic content, but on reflection I heard little about the kinds of difficulties I later encountered in the student group. I cannot tell whether this was because the student group was functioning exceptionally well at this point, or whether my probably somewhat idealized notions of how the students worked together precluded my thinking in terms of difficulties. Or maybe the student I met decided not to scare me off by revealing awkwardness. At the next stage, all the applicants met the whole student group and there was a discussion on a paper chosen by the student group. The prospect of this discussion was, for me, by far the most worrying aspect of the selection procedure, involving the risk of revealing vulnerable aspects of myself to others (some of whom I knew) who would be involved in the final decision on admissions. My anxiety was not relieved after receiving a copy of the paper to be discussed: Winnicott's 'Hate in the countertransference'. However, having recovered from the shock of the title, I actually enjoyed both reading the paper myself and then the discussion in the student group. Fears of not being up to understanding what was said or stating a point of view seemed to me to be exaggerated: I did get a lot out of the discussion, and felt pleased at being able to contribute what felt like relevant material from my own practice. The hard part was an awareness of issues raised by the presence of the other applicants. Would we all get in? If not, which of us would be acceptable? And would I be one of them? What would happen if I didn't say anything, or if I said something stupid, or too much? Fantasies around these questions stayed with me long after that meeting.

The interviews, held a week later, were more comfortable. I met first with one trained member, followed by a meeting with a student and a trained member. Both these meetings left me with a genuine feeling of being listened to and understood, with a view to trying to ascertain whether the Outfit would be right for me, as well as the other way around.

I was relieved to be accepted, and when I joined the student group I was nervous but excited to be there. The idea of belonging to a group of like-minded people engaged in a joint endeavour no doubt contained unrealistic and unexamined fantasies. My rational side, which knew enough about the possible snares involved in working within an unstructured group, was taken over by idealized expectations. The Outfit philosophy, so alluring and promising, tempted me to assume that all would now be well, that I would engage in a creative and nurturing process of becoming a psychotherapist. I have indeed become one and I believe the training has offered me the best possible opportunity to experience and examine those aspects of myself, both individually and in relation to others, that is necessary in order to emerge as a psychotherapist. But it has not been an easy training. The absence of both the authoritative parents and the well-defined task, the loneliness inevitably experienced at times during the training, the power of the unheld sibling group – all these perhaps represent the shadow side of the public image of the Outfit: the student-led, non-authoritative facilitating environment where students create their own training and facilitate the training of others, using the resources available from the trained group. Experiencing and working through difficulties inherent in the training has been, within the safety of my therapy, part of the foundation underpinning my work as a therapist. Personal and professional integration has followed from reconciling the reality and the idealizations, the group and the individual, the disappointments and the hopes, the envy and the reparation.

There were 12 members in the student group when I joined. This was an awkward size: too large for discussing papers, presenting case material or managing ourselves. I picked up soon enough that there had been some discussion on the possibility of splitting into smaller groups, but there seemed to be resistance to that idea. Worries to do with change, uncertainty, comparison and competition seemed to be around. Perhaps the very use of the word 'splitting' raised anxieties. In any event, it seemed impossible to talk about the implications of being in a group this size, or think together about what could be done. As a new member I was worried about how I would fit in, how others would experience me, whether I would come up to their expectations, and whether I would 'get it right', something difficult to hope for in the absence of clearly defined 'rules'. I found I could not understand what was going on in the group, and began to be aware of difficult feelings of powerlessness, anger and disappointment. There were things I wanted to say, or ask, but I could not find my voice. I began to take these feelings to my therapy and gradually became more conscious of the difficulties specific to me of being in this group. Much later, after more therapy and more experience of the group, I understood more about not only my own unconscious part, but the parts of others too, in powerful undercurrents that I think were to do with sibling rivalry, authority, responsibility, and envy. Living with, accepting and then moving on from powerful feelings like those is hard to achieve in a group that has no leader. Inevitably projections, transferences, and countertransferences fly around in a flurry of anguished confusion. I missed the safety of the parental holding I had experienced in a previous group. I could not find the strength, or certainty, or words to express myself and so I became part of the confusion. Monday evenings lost their excitement and I lost my enthusiasm and the training became a burden. I felt awful about myself and wondered why I was so angry, why I was finding it so difficult to concentrate on the academic content, why I was feeling so isolated and confused. These inevitable reactions to membership in a group were, I think, confounded by the interconnection between the size of the group, the absence of a leader and the evident inability of the group to confront the dynamics. I am sure I was not alone in feeling like this, and I think there was some discussion about these issues on an individual level. But still the student group remained stuck as a frightening and difficult place for some time.

Things did, however, improve. There was some discussion and acknowledgement within the group of a need to address the dynamics. Perhaps the mere acknowledgement of this made us all feel better. There was a shared feeling that the group was too large and together we worked out how to rearrange ourselves. The new arrangement involved the whole student group meeting together at the start of the evening to make plans and arrangements before breaking up into three smaller groups. I certainly felt much freer in discussing papers, presenting case material and talking about training as a psychotherapist in this new context, and I believe that was a shared experience. Insights obtained in therapy, conversations with some of my trained and student pairs, and a growing confidence in myself as a therapist as I began working, all contributed to a greater acceptance and enjoyment of the student group as something that could be good enough, if not perfect. There were subsequently other distressing and awkward times in the group and I imagine that is an inevitable part of the training. But accepting the responsibility of recognizing and addressing those difficulties and then keeping on going has, for me, been a valuable part of the Outfit training.

I do not want to imply that the student group was only difficult and distressing. Far from it. I have experienced genuine expressions of interest and concern on both personal and Outfit issues, and I have been aware of others also receiving group support. There have been many occasions of intellectual excitement and engagement, of common expressions of confusion and doubt, as well as times of playful hilarity. We even managed some creativity when reorganizing the structure of the group, or when deciding what themes to take on and how to do them, or when realizing that by meeting half an hour earlier we could thereby get rid of our business and still have the same length of time for psychotherapy. I have found membership of the student group a complicated, challenging, often uncomfortable but ultimately enriching experience.

The system of 'pairings', so distinctive to the Outfit, provided an opportunity to get to know, and be known by, other members. As the Outfit has grown, this system has helped members make and maintain contact with each other. At the beginning, meetings with my trained and student pairs enabled me to find things out, ask questions and explain myself in an intimate context. Early meetings with my student pairs were a good chance to find out more about what being a student really meant and what was involved, and also about some of the ongoing issues that I hadn't picked up. I gained enormously from these meetings, both personally and as a developing psychotherapist. Inevitably there was often talk about personal therapy, clinical work and supervision and, once again, issues of envy and rivalry were sometimes present. In my experience, these difficult issues were rarely talked about in the pairing but sometimes provided rich material for therapy.

When it came to meeting my trained pair, as a 'youngster' in the Outfit I both wanted and expected, the first few times, to be contacted by my trained pair. It was only when I realized that it didn't always work like that that I began to recognize my responsibility in making a pair happen, and that, of course, involved me recognizing how much I still yearned to be looked after by a figure of authority. Being called a 'student' carried a suggestion for me of being somewhat irresponsible, of being cared for, of not needing to take decisions and these seemed attractive possibilities for someone of my age and stage in life. Taking on this responsibility felt both good and adult, but there was also the sadness and loss involved in growing up. Initially, meetings with my trained pair sometimes evoked feelings of anxiety about being judged, but the subsequent diminishing of those feelings and a greater freedom to use the meetings more creatively to talk about psychotherapy suggested that I was finding my place in the Outfit.

Being a student entailed a greater time commitment than I had perhaps foreseen. Personal therapy, membership of the student group, supervised clinical work and meetings in pairs – I had known about and accepted all this. I suppose I must have been informed when I applied about the quarterly business meetings at which the Outfit, as a collective, makes decisions and carries them out. However, I was somewhat taken aback when informed of the first business meeting and can only surmise that I had 'chosen' to ignore the need to engage in this manner. My memories of the first few business meetings I attended are dominated by two themes. Firstly, it never occurred to me in any way that I might need, want, or be expected to take an active part in the business of the Outfit. That was, I assumed, going to be taken care of by other more senior, experienced and knowledgeable members. Secondly, the possibility of my actually saying anything in this august and rather frightening forum seemed remote. There seemed to be far too many parental figures around for me to feel like taking any risks. The gradual process of accepting some responsibility for the care and development of the Outfit, and feeling confident enough to contribute to discussion, reflected my ongoing personal growth through therapy. My fear and diffidence in speaking at business meetings was also present, of course, at the joint monthly meetings of both student and trained members at which psychotherapeutic topics are discussed. Recognizing the inevitability of growing up, and the losses and gains associated with it, and also being able to recognize and receive signs of acceptance and regard has led to greater participation in a group that once seemed so awesome.

The idea of graduation, that process of growth from student to real grown-up psychotherapist, was not in my mind when I embarked on the training. How pleasant it was to be free of those concerns associated with 'growing up'! That freedom is something particular to the Outfit, since there is no prescribed manner or timeframe for graduation. I was aware, of course, when I joined, that there had been some recent graduations but those were 'out there', not something to do with me. I was more connected to the first few graduations after I joined but I am ashamed, as I look back, that my sense of responsibility for engaging in each graduation was slow to develop. Inevitably the issue of my own graduation began dimly to emerge. I remember one day being rather unexpectedly conscious of the fact that a time would come when I would want to consider the idea more carefully and then announce my intention. It still seemed a long way off. When I started talking more about the eventual reality of my graduation in supervision and therapy I realized that I had, in a sense, actively started my graduation process. What had up to then been an intellectual understanding of what gradu-ation meant became a deeply personal engagement with a process that involved opening myself to a fairly public scrutiny. I suppose by this time I must have felt strong and certain enough, for I decided to write a personal and open account of myself, thinking that this was the most honest way of presenting myself to the Outfit. This seemed rather a risky thing to do as it was entirely different from my previously more careful, structured and academic ways of doing things, and it involved an uncertain response. I assumed that not all members would have the time or commitment to engage deeply with me, and I knew that others probably knew my work and me well enough. I wanted to offer the possibility to anyone who wanted to challenge me, support me or disagree with me. As it happened, the responses and discussions I had were supportive and enriching.

As the Outfit has become larger, it has almost inevitably laid itself open to difficulties, and changing needs can be difficult to identify and explore in the democratic and non-authoritarian milieu. This dilemma can be understood within the context of graduation, in which great emphasis has traditionally been placed on students presenting themselves for graduation in their own personal and creative manner. While this has worked well within a relatively small and cohesive group, it seems to be a very much more complicated process to undertake in the increasingly large Outfit. Thought and discussion will have to be given to this, and other far-reaching and probably unforeseen con-sequences of expansion.

Training in the Outfit is a difficult option for the kinds of reasons I have described. Trying to grow in the absence of 'parents'; living with and trying to understand the negativity sometimes present in the student group; internalizing the culture of the Outfit; finding one's own authenticity: I cannot imagine I am the only student who has found it hard at times to be certain about what I was doing. My struggle with these issues was unexpectedly difficult, often unwelcome and sometimes demoralizing and exhausting. But having won through and having survived leaves me with a sense of understanding and empower-ment. My personal sense of victory and achievement would be dimin-ished had I not had to face up to my own responsibility in developing into the therapist I am now. The military metaphors in the last sentences imply, quite accurately, that the training did sometimes feel like a battle. But not all the time. Between the skirmishes there were long periods of calm productivity interspersed with patches of lively and creative fun. And it certainly helped having a 'good' therapist with whom I could mull over my confusions and conflicts. Especially a therapist who understood something about the Outfit.

* * * * *

Throughout my training I was seeing Peter for therapy two or three times a week. This inevitably raised interesting questions and dilemmas for me, although I believe it is a familiar situation for Peter to find himself in. Could I be absolutely certain about confidentiality? Would Peter find out things about me from other Outfit sources? How would my therapy with Peter affect my relationship with other students? Should I be concerned about envy rearing its ugly head? Would I be strong enough to find my own therapeutic style or would the influence of 'the great man', as I jokingly referred to him, be too much?

At first, my emotional reactions to seeing Peter at Outfit meetings subsumed anything else that I wanted, or was expected to do. His presence was huge and overwhelming and paralysing. I worried about how he would be experiencing me in that context, not wanting, perhaps, to shatter a particular image of myself that I was presenting to him in therapy. I certainly felt unable to speak, assuming I would be judged by him as I had by others. I looked out for little signs that he noticed me, and felt rivalrous of others when I observed them in conversation with him. Addressing these and other powerful reactions to seeing him interact with others offered me more personal insight, I believe, than if my therapy and training had not overlapped. The first Outfit Christmas party I attended provides a good example. Surrounded by others apparently having a reasonably good time, I felt mesmerized by his presence. Should I say 'hello' to him, or would it be better to avoid him? I managed, I think, to maintain my poise fairly well, my determination to join the activities belying the inner turmoil. However, even my poise was stretched to the limit when it was announced that we would all play musical chairs. My fantasies went into overdrive, culminating in imagining that Peter and I would be engaged in fighting it out for the last chair. Or perhaps we would share the last chair, and I would sit on his lap. And so it went on . . . I took the only possible course open to me and fled. It should not be difficult to imagine the wealth of material that incident provided for my therapy.

Themes addressed in therapy wove in and out of issues involved in training and it seems impossible to know which influenced what. Initially I found it difficult to accept the absence of 'rules' in therapy and struggled to make use of the freedom that offered. At the same time I was confronting the issue of personal responsibility in creating my own training in the absence of 'rules'. I had occasion at times in my training to hear Peter praised or criticized. Sometimes I was asked to carry messages between students and Peter. Seemingly insignificant incidents like these provided ample material for the therapeutic work as well as helping me define my place in the training. Since there were other students also in therapy with Peter, issues relating to sibling rivalry were present within the training context, but were rarely and even then inadequately addressed between students or within the student group.

However, confronting and addressing these and similar issues in therapy not only clarified significant personal concerns but also enabled me to understand better what goes on in groups in general, as well as more specifically in both student and large Outfit groups.

As the therapy progressed, my idealization of Peter began slowly to diminish. Our relationship became more ordinary, or realistic, and exactly because of that it became a better and richer relationship, capable of greater intimacy. My idealized notions of what the Outfit training could offer me, or indeed what being a psychotherapist entailed, similarly began to diminish, though I cannot tell which way the symbiotic process was working at that point. What was clear was that my expectations of both therapy and training had become more realistic, and I was getting more out of each of them.

As I moved towards, and then beyond, graduation, so my relationship with Peter has changed. My dependence on his presence as 'the great man' has diminished and in its place is a warmer, easier, and friendlier companionship. The fact that I have not discussed this chapter with him, as I have previously with other pieces of writing, is due not only to my wish to give him a present but also suggests an increased sense of independence. Therapeutic issues are talked about in our sessions but much time is also spent discussing films and art exhibitions, or chewing over contemporary moral issues. Clearly the time will come when I no longer visit him in need of therapy. What kind of relationship then emerges remains to be seen.

When I saw Peter's austere figure slowly climbing the stairs to the meeting that was about to recognize my graduation, I was struck by the extraordinary nature and power of the relationship that had developed between us. This man was coming to a meeting of an organization he had set up, although he hardly ever attends such meetings nowadays. Whether that is because he feels too old, or too lazy, or is too deaf; who knows? I knew at that moment that he had come because he understood that I wanted him to be there. And he was there for me.

Chapter 4
Common humanity

LUCY KING

I first came across Peter Lomas's ideas about psychotherapy when I read *True and False Experience* nearly 25 years ago. I felt immediately attracted to his approach to therapy: its directness, its lack of jargon, its obvious humaneness. Some time later when I embarked on psychotherapy training with the Philadelphia Association, I asked Peter, who had fairly recently moved to Cambridge, if he would supervise me. I remain extremely grateful that he said yes. Not only did he become my principal supervisor during my training (and after) but we have been colleagues in the 'Outfit' (the Cambridge Society for Psychotherapy) ever since it first emerged out of discussions between Peter and David Ingleby in 1980.

In this essay I want to discuss a number of interlinked themes that run through Peter Lomas's work and which have been important to me in my development as a psychotherapist. First, his belief that psychotherapy training should not be primarily concerned with imparting theoretical knowledge or techniques. Rather, it should be an enabling process through which trainees learn to draw on their own personal qualities and life experiences, in combination with the insights and experiences of others, in order to evolve therapeutically effective ways of being with, and responding to, people in distress. Second, his encouragement of people to find their own style and voice as therapists. Third, his approval of careful reading and reflection on psychoanalytic theory without allowing it to become a defensive barrier preventing one from being fully alive to what is being said or not said between therapist and client. Fourth, his emphasis on the value of the ordinary human qualities of the therapist, and his reminder of what is lost if we concentrate too exclusively on transference, and neglect simpler interpersonal aspects of the therapeutic relationship.

Thinking about what characterizes my experience of supervision with Peter, I find myself being drawn back repeatedly to a cluster of Winnicott's ideas about child development. In particular, the concept of the facilitating environment (Winnicott, 1965), and the idea of the baby as a 'going concern' (Winnicott, 1964). I later came across Wyn Bramley's description of the supervisory couple having parallels with Winnicott's nursing couple (Bramley, 1996). In each case, both members of the couple are equally and actively involved in development. Neither can achieve it in isolation from the other.

The idea of the baby as a going concern embodies the belief *not* that babies can survive and grow on their own but that, given a satisfactory human and material environment, they contain within themselves the potential for growth towards maturity. The role of the (m)other is to facilitate the unfolding of that potential. Similarly, trainee therapists may be encouraged to develop their therapeutic qualities, their ability to listen to, and to withstand, the distress that their patients bring to them.

The 'good enough' (m)other is present and solicitous but allows sufficient distance to foster the gradual emergence of the infant's awareness of its separateness. A facilitating environment is not overly watchful or protective. Impingement can be as damaging or inhibiting as neglect. In True and False Experience Peter writes of patients who have been too anxiously watched as children and have not been given sufficient freedom to be or to grow (Lomas, 1973: 62 and 127).

Supervision as a facilitating environment can be seen as a place (or space) in which all trainees' sense of themselves as developing therapists is nurtured and encouraged. This does not preclude criticism or careful attention to limits and boundaries, but the emphasis remains supportive and affirming. In supervision with Peter I have never felt put down. I have felt sufficiently safe to admit mistakes and confusion. Criticism has come generally in the form of quite gently making me aware how my own neurotic patterns might be hampering my ability to help my clients. My sense is that I have become more aware of both my strengths and weaknesses as a therapist, and this has helped me to avoid defensively blocking what a client might be struggling to communicate. He has helped me gain confidence and hence the capacity to withstand the intensity of both negative and positive (idealizing) transferences. I have also got somewhat better at judging what I can and cannot effectively cope with. Perhaps more importantly, I have acquired at least some confidence that it is all right to act on this. My experience is well described in the following passage from *Cultivating Intuition:*

> a good training is one that allows and encourages the student to trust, as far as possible, his own intuitive capacity and to build on his own style of being with people rather than suppressing it and replacing it with a formula for behaviour imposed from without. (Lomas, 1994: 136–7)

In contrast to this attitude, much psychotherapy and psychotherapy training seems beset by a sort of machismo. There is a covert, or sometimes overt, emphasis on power and authority. The style is of potent, penetrating interpretations. Facilitation is not macho. It invokes a more containing way of being that encourages the person's own capacity to explore, learn and develop. As Winnicott emphasized, the most effective interpretations are made by patients themselves. A facilitative approach allows the development of a person's own style, the ability to be themselves rather than having goals and values imposed on them. As Harold Searles puts it, 'the other person must be left to find that road to Rome which is most in keeping with his own capacities and interests' (Searles, 1965: 586).

It is a little ironic to suggest an analogy between Peter Lomas's ideas on psychotherapy training, and child development, as he places great emphasis on the fact that psychotherapy students are mature adults with considerable and varied life experiences. He deplores the way that they are often made to feel not just novices in this field but quasi-juveniles as well. One of the main thrusts of his criticism of psychoanalysis, which is equally true of psychotherapy training, is that whereas it may aim to increase autonomy, confidence and maturity, the techniques used can have the opposite effect and be infantilizing. This is not to belittle the value of regression as part of a therapeutic process, or to imply that child-like as well as more adult modes of being should not be in play. Peter in fact notes in *True and False Experience* that whereas Freud underestimates the adult in the patient, Carl Rogers underestimates the child. Both show lack of respect for the nature of the child and an idealized view of adult self-control (Lomas, 1973: 81).

Peter's preferred model of learning to be a psychotherapist conforms to his ideas about the practice of psychotherapy more generally: that it is a co-operative activity aiming to increase insight and foster both autonomy and the ability to interact closely with others. It involves the therapist and client reflecting together on the client's life and exploring the ways in which it is blocked, rigidified or impoverished. Learning to be a psychotherapist can be seen as a developmental process, a cultivation of sensibilities and ways of being with people, as much as the acquiring of theoretical knowledge and understanding. I am deliberately using the word learning here rather than training, as training has somewhat authoritarian associations and also implies something that is given to people (or dogs!). 'Learning' puts the emphasis on the person who is learning rather than on the trainer/teacher. Peter's ideas about learning are very much student-centred.

Throughout his writings he has emphasized the importance of the client being regarded with respect as an equal human being, that is, not being invalidated through being either pathologized or infantilized. It goes with this that the relationship between therapist and client is of central importance and that the nature of this relationship is, as far as possible, an intersubjective, 'I–thou' one rather than a subject-object, 'I–it' one. This is not to ignore the many factors that make it difficult to achieve this, but to stress the importance of minimizing rather than augmenting them. The therapist–client relationship is not a reciprocal one and there are almost bound to be power inequalities in such an asymmetrical relationship. People seeking help from a therapist are likely to feel vulnerable and exposed. Techniques that play on and exploit this vulnerability and emphasize the power and authority of the therapist may be effective in encouraging certain sorts of parental transferences but this does not necessarily help the therapy:

> The more the analyst's technique and behaviour are suggestive of omniscience and omnipotence, the greater is the danger of a malignant form of regression. On the other hand, the more the analyst can reduce the inequality between his patient and himself, the more unobtrusive and ordinary he can remain in his patient's eyes, the better are the chances of a benign form of regression. (Balint, 1979: 173)

In *Cultivating Intuition*, Peter Lomas talks of the importance of supervisor and student being given comparable status, the difference between them being only one of experience. Of course, greater experience may give greater confidence and there may also be power differentials that need to be acknowledged in order to minimize their hampering the working relationship.

Student psychotherapists, despite being mature adults, are also susceptible to becoming somewhat regressed, or infantilized. They are usually immersed in their own training therapy. All sorts of issues arising in this may be making them vulnerable and dependant. Placing oneself in the role of student and struggling with difficult and perhaps unfamiliar concepts can also make one feel de-skilled and prey to all sorts of uncertainties and insecurities. On top of this, clinical supervision, although hopefully supportive and helpful, involves exposing one's mistakes and incompetences, leaving one open to potentially humiliating criticism. It is very hard for a trainee not to become narcissistically entangled with a client's therapeutic progress. It is easy to become desperate to say the right thing or to devise a clever interpretation, and to become anxious that one will be found wanting and not good enough.

As Harold Searles observes (Searles, 1965: 589), it is rarely useful for a supervisor merely to point out how the therapist *should* have responded. This just leaves them feeling inadequate and stupid. It is much more likely to be helpful to explore what might have been happening in the interaction that made it difficult for the therapist to respond. Having said that, however, I well recall that as a trainee I often longed to be put out of my agony and just told how to do it! Peter often in fact said very little, yet I almost always felt clearer about what was going on, even if not always much nearer knowing quite how to proceed in the next session with the client.

In his article on psychoanalytic supervision, Searles, too, uses a Winnicottian image: that of the mother holding the baby while the father 'holds', or in some sense protects, the nursing couple (Searles, 1965: 595). I have considerable reservations about Winnicott's delimiting the paternal role in this way, but it does seem an appropriate model for aspects of the supervisor–therapist–client triad. In *Boundary and Space* Davis and Wallbridge (1983) write of the necessity of maintaining the circle made by the father or father substitute in order to allow the mother to abandon herself to the infant's needs without anxiety. In the family, the protection may be provided literally and materially. In the case of therapeutic supervision it can only be symbolic as the supervisor is not present in the therapy session. It can, none the less, feel a powerful support.

Searles points out that just as a large part of a therapist's usefulness to the patient is a consequence of being outside their life and therefore having a different perspective, a large part of the potential usefulness of supervisors is their even greater emotional distance from the patient. This may enable them to see things that the therapist/student may overlook. Searles maintains that the value of the supervisor is not to do with being more intelligent or intuitive – merely about having a different perspective. The greater emotional distance results in relatively little anxiety and consequently it may seem as if there is more space to think clearly and creatively.

One characteristic that distinguishes Peter Lomas' attitude towards therapy, supervision and training from much psychoanalytic psychotherapy, is that he does not see therapy as dominated by the need to overcome resistances. Therefore, therapeutic encounters are not envisaged as battles. There is no need constantly to avoid being outmanoeuvred. Nor is there excessive anxiety about collusion or seemingly paranoid fears of being manipulated. Psychoanalysis can easily acquire a distinctly paranoid tinge, a tendency to ruminate obsessively on 'what is *really* going on'. What am I failing to see behind a seemingly innocent word or action? Such questioning can have value but it can also become counterproductive.

My remarks here about Peter's refreshingly straightforward approach might appear to imply that he has a rather rosy, even sentimental, view of life, but this is not the case. He startled me once by recalling having agreed with a despairing client about the miserableness of life. The crucial thing is that with Peter there is a sense of being in this awfulness together, as allies. Psychotherapy *can* be a struggle but this therapeutic alliance means that it is not a matter of therapist and client lined up against each other as combatants on opposing sides. This is not to deny that therapeutic interactions can sometimes seem like desperate struggles, and of course people can be resistant or sabotage the therapy. They can be self-deceptive, manipulative or difficult to be with in any number of ways. But the optimal default position is not necessarily to keep at a safe distance. It is sometimes precisely when one does get caught up or taken in to some degree, that one begins to understand what is at stake.

One consequence of this relative freedom from therapeutic paranoia is that therapeutic interactions are not bristling with anxieties about the boundaries within and around them. There is a lot of talk and concern amongst therapists and counsellors about personal and professional boundaries. An important aspect of the therapeutic encounter is, indeed, that it is bounded in space and time. The regularity and reliability of these limits gives a sense of security and a consequent freedom to speak or to remain silent. Psychoanalytic psychotherapy sessions in fact have very little structure other than this constraint in space and time.

Boundaries, however, may be of different sorts. They may be rigid and fortified or, like cell membranes in the human body, they may be semi-permeable. Therapeutic boundaries too can be multi-purpose: strong enough to form reliable containers and give structure and stability, but permeable and flexible enough to allow free interchange in both verbal and non-verbal, conscious and non-conscious registers.

Some of the variation in psychotherapists' attitudes to boundaries is related to the type of psychotherapy involved, the rigidity of the boundaries reflecting (or being inversely correlated with) the internal structure of the therapy. Thus, practitioners of highly structured therapies such as those employing cognitive and behavioural techniques, may be relatively little bothered by anxieties about personal boundaries. Person-centred therapists, on the other hand, tend to lay fastidious emphasis in their training on the maintenance of 'professional' boundaries. Such differences in attitude would follow the pattern described by Mary Douglas in *Purity and Danger* (1970). Taboos, rules and rituals that keep the sexes apart are stronger and more prevalent in societies where structural gender-role differentiation is weaker.

I suspect, however, that this does not give a complete picture and that the setting and maintenance of boundaries may owe as much to personal style as to theoretical orientation. Therapists, as much as clients, may, as individuals, be more or less fearful of possible intrusion, engulfment, or merging. Ernest Jones was said to have refused to have shaken hands with his patients on the grounds that what they really wanted to shake was his penis. One may ask whose fantasy this was – his or the patient's?

As I said earlier, learning to be a psychotherapist involves developing, over a considerable number of years, a way of being with people in distress, and this must be a matter of individual style as much as adherence to any particular body of theory. Not that theory and personal style are as separable as that may seem to imply. I very much doubt that anyone chooses the theory they work with on purely intellectual grounds. We surely all work best in a manner that suits us personally.

One in which we feel comfortable and that allows us in some sense 'to be ourselves'. This may influence both our choice of theoretical position and how we adapt it to ourselves.

Thinking on these lines about some of my psychotherapy colleagues, it is obvious that in this matching of personal to theoretical style there may also be elements of compensation in a rather Jungian sense. People are usually somewhat different in their consulting rooms than they customarily are outside them. Being a therapist may have enabled them to explore and utilize certain aspects or capacities that are much less emphasized elsewhere in their lives. For instance, I puzzled for a while about why an aquaintance had chosen to become a Kleinian therapist and who talked of someone's, to my mind fairly minor, self-disclosure as 'professional malpractice'. My puzzle was that this aquaintance seemed so *far*, temperamentally, from anything remotely resembling a 'blank screen'. Then I realized that this was the point. Here was someone who needed the discipline of the Kleinian attitude to curtail the force of his personal presence and his tendency to take up most of the space in a dialogue. The emphasis on interpretation still allowed him to display his sharp intelligence and put it to good advantage.

Peter Lomas, in contrast, has a rather restrained and austere demeanor. He is not someone who seems likely to become either too chatty or wildly self-revealing. One could be fairly certain that he could safely give the occasional cup of coffee to a client without becoming alarmingly over-familiar or intrusive. Personal revelation from him is more likely to be felt as a gift than an unwelcome impingement.

We have come to take for granted the differences between the various schools of psychotherapy and tend to assume that they have arisen for primarily clinical or theoretical reasons, whereas they are, at least partially, the consequence of temperamental differences between the founding fathers that have later become elevated into doctrine. The use of the analytic couch evolved from the instructions that Freud gave to his earliest psychotherapy patients in order to cover his discomfort over his poor hypnotic skills (Breuer and Freud, 1895: 107–11). Later, in his Papers on Technique, the first reason that Freud gave for continuing with this arrangement was that he disliked being stared at all day (Freud, 1913: 134). Jung, who advocated sitting eyeball-to-eyeball with his patients, was clearly much happier with a more direct, face-to-face interaction.

Freud further explains his preference for remaining out of sight behind the patient's head, by saying:

> Since while I am listening to the patient, I, too, give myself over to the current of my unconscious thoughts, I do not wish my expressions of face to give the patient material for interpretations or to influence him in what he tells me. (Freud, 1913: 134)

The familiar and orthodox Freudian prescription for the analytic relationship is that it should be without content. The analyst should be a blank screen on to which the analysand projects feelings that arise from past experiences and not primarily from his actual interaction with the analyst. Freud advocated the cultivation of 'reserve' on the part of the analyst; an analytic attitude of neutrality in which the person of the analyst is not allowed to intrude or interfere. The implication of his description of his need to remain out of sight, is that while this 'neutrality' may be a desirable impression to give the patient, what might be going on for the analyst might well be quite different.

Psychoanalytic neutrality can perhaps be regarded as equivalent to so-called scientific objectivity. This is now widely acknowledged to be inevitably incomplete, if not entirely mythical. Even if one wants to retain neutrality as an ideal to be aimed at, any presumption of it can be misleading and mystifying. As Eric Rayner puts it:

> All analysts have different styles of emotionality, these are often known by patients and it is best to recognize this. There is no such thing as sterile analysing. The quiet emotionality of the analyst is the milieu or ground upon which the patient develops his own expressiveness. (Rayner, 1991: 289–90)

Apart from anything else, neutrality is as likely to be interpreted or misinterpreted as any other response. One morning recently, two consecutive student clients coincidentally started their sessions by reporting their impressions of my attitude to them. The first said how much she felt that I was 'on her side'. The second, complained that I never gave any indication of what I thought of her. I was unaware of acting or, indeed feeling, any more friendly or warm to one than the other.

Being non-judgmental towards people seeking our help is generally considered desirable and to be striven for. It is equally the case that people will at times feel judged whatever one's good intentions. Silent neutrality, however genuine, can be experienced as disapproval or even persecution. Psychoanalysis advocates an analytic attitude of neutrality. Carl Rogers and other person-centred therapists speak of the necessity for a therapeutic attitude of 'unconditional positive regard'. Both stances can be translucent masks covering, or failing to cover, a whole mêlée of responses, both conscious and unconscious.

Even if one does not want to pull down the entire edifice of analytic neutrality, it seems vital to acknowledge its, or our, limitations. Gregory Bateson wrote of the maddening effect of a parent who gives contradictory messages. For example, by telling a child that they love them while acting in ways that convey precisely the opposite (Bateson, 1973: 173–98). It may be similarly damaging for a therapist not to own up to certain emotional responses, especially when someone clearly suspects their existence. It is all too easy and tempting to divert attention away by an interpretation, implying that they are mistaken in their perceptions. We require honesty of our patients, and their shortcomings in this regard are interpreted as resistance. We take rather too little notice of the resistances of the therapist.

A number of well-known and experienced psychoanalysts have spoken of occasions on which they lapsed from their habitual, overtly detached stance. Symington described such occasions as 'the Analyst's Act of Freedom' (Symington, 1986). They have sometimes been breakthroughs as well as break-outs, and have released an analytic process that had become stuck. Nina Coltart gave an example of this in *Slouching towards Bethlehem: or thinking the unthinkable in Psychoanalysis* (Symington, 1986) Here she talked of shouting in rage after months of impenetrable silence that suddenly felt like murderous hatred. The shouting acted as a break for freedom for both analyst and patient. In the same paper she said how she later regretted that, as a trainee anxious to obey the sacred rules, she had restrained herself from laughing when analysing a very funny man. She eventually came to feel that in doing so she might have suffocated something in the patient, herself, and the analytic process (Coltart, 1986: 185 and197).

One important point about such incidents of rule breaking is that they are just that: incidents of rule breaking. Isolated moments of emotionality that serve to break a deadlock. Their apparent effectiveness lies in their shock value, their great and sudden contrast with the usual progress of the analysis. Furthermore, they are therapeutically successful lapses. I suspect many (if not most) therapists could also recall moments when they have 'lost it'. Some of these come eventually to feel useful, while some continue to be remembered as guilt-provoking instances of retaliation – what Winnicott might describe as a momentary 'failure to survive' as therapists, even if the failure is not complete and the therapeutic relationship recovers.

In contrast to this, in arguing against the ideal of neutrality, Peter Lomas's emphasis is not on occasional break-outs but on a more personal style of being that suffuses the whole therapeutic relationship. It is an emphasis on the value of being present as a fellow human being and not just as something resembling a stone wall over which the patient drapes projections. In this, Peter stands somewhat apart not just from the psychoanalytic mainstream but from the position of the humanistic therapist Carl Rogers as well. He points out that, whereas Rogers believes that therapists and counsellors should be warm and empathic, they should also remain calm and unemotional. Peter, on the other hand, writes:

> While accepting that it is sometimes necessary to conceal ones' own anxiety when confronted by panic, it seems to me that a consistently unemotional attitude opens up a gap between two people – the patient is likely to feel inferior in the face of such self-control. (Lomas, 1981: 80)

As well as advocating a more emotionally open way of responding to people in therapy, Peter wants to encourage a more immediate and personal, rather than theory-dominated, pattern of therapeutic interaction:

> Contemporary psychotherapy proposes a framework of theory within which the practitioner may, to a certain degree, reveal ordinary human qualities. By contrast, I would suggest that psychotherapy is the manifestation of creative human qualities in a facilitative setting in which the task of healing is eased by a critical knowledge of the theories and teaching of twentieth-century practictioners. (Lomas, 1981: 3)

The exact place of theory and theorizing within psychotherapy training has been, and continues to be, in some ways an even thornier issue than its place within therapy itself. Peter himself has been derided in some quarters for supposedly championing the idea of 'ordinary housewives' becoming therapists. This is taken to imply that psychotherapy is something that just *anyone* can do, more or less off the street or out of the kitchen. I think that this misunderstands Peter's point, which is to emphasize that psychotherapy is not a purely intellectual activity requiring primarily academic and technical skills, but is, rather, about the development of the ability to be with, to listen, and respond to people in emotional turmoil and distress. It is not that candidates for psychotherapy training should not be carefully selected. Nor that they do not benefit from prolonged and arduous training. It certainly does not mean that psychotherapy is merely about tea and sympathy, or that there is no place for theoretical concepts or critical thought.

Embedded in this is the belief, shared, of course, by many psychotherapists, that therapy is essentially about relationship, about dialogue, about what goes on between the two people in the consulting room. It is not fundamentally about imparting knowledge or practising techniques. Therefore, to cultivate intellectual knowledge while disregarding other, less formally teachable qualities, is to underplay the crucial importance of quite ordinary human attributes such as attentiveness, honesty, courage and reliability. Moreover, as Peter points out, failures of therapy are not so much failures of technique, as ordinary human ones such as confusion, rigidity, over-anxiety, rejection, or indifference – the inability to 'be there' for the patient in whatever way is called for (Lomas, 1973: 93).

Peter's approach downplays, but does not completely reject, theory. It embodies the belief that theories should arise as reflections on, or attempts to make sense of, clinical experiences, as opposed to practice being conducted within a preordained theoretical framework. The difficulty is how to teach people to think critically while neither dismissing nor idealizing theoretical concepts. There is some force to the argument that, far from being untainted by scholasticism, 'ordinary housewives' may be intimidated by theory and therefore become in thrall to it (John Heaton, private communication). Theories are not infectious diseases, but their influence can be quite insidious. Someone like Peter, with the benefit of both medical and psychoanalytic trainings behind him, can perhaps more easily allow theoretical ideas to rest lightly upon him.

Theory can be enlightening. It can also be mystifying or defensive or comforting. It can provide a way of avoiding feeling unbearably vulnerable to assault by the unmediated anguish or confusion that people bring to us. It may sometimes seem a necessary defence. Defence mechanisms provide our everyday means of coping with anxiety, as well as having the potential to become *ab*normal and unhealthy limitations on our lives. Theory can be an effective way of structuring our reflections on what is going on between therapist and client. It can act as a map or guide – and, as with good guidebooks, it can help us observe notable features that we might otherwise overlook. On the other hand, if we have our noses stuck in our guidebooks we might fail to notice other equally important things. These might include the general life and atmosphere around us. Furthermore, the sort of guidebook that theory provides is a general rather than specific one. It is like a general guide to Romanesque churches, for example. The particular church that we find ourselves in may have some of the features described but is unlikely to have *all* of them. Trying to fit it rigidly into the expected schema may completely distort our perception of it.

A recurrent dilemma in teaching or learning psychotherapy, is how to use the wealth of insight and wisdom that has built up within the field of psychoanaysis in a way that enriches our developing practice rather than blinkering it. For example, Infant Observation under the direction of an experienced therapist can be a fascinating and valuable opportunity to learn from them. It is an integral part of many trainings and available as a supplement to others. It, however, teaches people to see infant behaviour and infant-mother interaction within a particular theoretical framework. As such it is not a neutral or objective activity. It can indoctrinate as well as enlighten. This is a dilemma that is not easy to resolve. It is more a matter of keeping in mind that there are potential pitfalls as well as benefits.

For Peter, a vital aspect of therapy is that in some very important sense it is an *ordinary* activity and the therapist is there as an ordinary person. For instance, a smile may be as powerful as a cleverly worded interpretation. Yet it is equally true, as I have already said, that part of the value of therapists is that they do not belong to the person's everyday life. They stand outside it. They are neither friend nor family in the strict sense, though they may come to feel in some ways like both. The therapeutic conversation, however intimate the content, is circumscribed by the rituals of time and setting. Perhaps it is for this very reason that it is essential for the therapist not to lose sight of his or her ordinariness, and for therapy trainings to help the trainees to avoid taking up false roles. One may have to endure being seen as the 'one who is supposed to know' (Lacan cited by Roustang, 1982: 18) but it is vital to avoid taking up a position as the one who *actually* knows.

One striking assertion that Peter Lomas makes is that ordinariness is an achievement (Lomas, 1994: 186). Failure to achieve it can drive individuals to compensate by seeking special and exclusive relationships. They then depend on these relationships for their self-esteem and confidence. As a consequence, they may feel that they have to display certain special qualities that (they believe) are appreciated by their significant other(s). If they come to doubt that they really possess these particular qualities, their self-esteem may feel very precarious and fragile.

I have repeatedly heard psychotherapy colleagues commenting on how important they have found it to be seen as ordinary, when working with clients from outside the middle-class intelligentsia. However, I find these ideas about ordinariness extremely pertinent in a different way in my work in and around Cambridge University.

Students and academics are frequently plagued by both sides of a paradox. On the one hand, they complain that they have never fitted in at school or elsewhere. That they were made to feel 'different' and marginalized or even bullied as a result. For some, this seems to have been the consequence of being academically able. For others, their academic pursuits allowed them to retreat from a social world that left them feeling incompetent, into a more comfortable world of abstraction or virtual reality. On the other hand, they have often internalized an imperative to be 'special' and to excel. They very often feel that their specialness is their only possible source of value. To be loved they must not just be good but the best, the very best. To be ordinary is to be mediocre, and this is equivalent to failure. Colleges encourage this by rewarding people who obtain the top grades in exams, and making quite clear their disapproval of those who only just pass. Achievement, moreover, is never final. There is always the *next* exam or essay, lecture or paper in which their fearfully anticipated 'real' mediocrity may be exposed. They are often beset by a terror of being 'found out' and rejected as not good enough, and consequently forfeiting the love and respect that they fear that they only fraudulently enjoy. Every piece of work therefore, can be an agony. Often it can seem worse to hand in something less than perfect, than not to hand in anything. Hidden behind an apparent lack of diligence can be fear-driven procrastination.

Achieving what was once felt to be the ultimate goal of an Oxbridge place (a goal that may have been their's or their parent's or their school's) may only increase the burdens of expectation on them. It may feel harder to be special here, while at the same time being just as terrifying merely to be one of the crowd. They bring with them their sense of shame and personal inadequacy; their failure to achieve ordinary things like love and friendship; their precarious, performance-dependent, self-esteem. They very often feel that they have lost much of what they previously took for granted: the attention and kudos of being 'top of the class'; the satisfaction of finding work easy; the envious admiration from peers. On top of all this is often a sense that, having got here, they are expected not just to do well but to be having a wonderful time. Being a student is supposed to be when you have 'the time of your life'.

If things become bad enough for them to seek counselling, then they may come needing to impress and engage the counsellor in intellectual discussions. They may be covertly, even overtly, contemptuous or competitive. They may demand that they see the 'best' therapist or analyst or that they are treated as special. Others may present themselves as the good and compliant client. This is hardly surprising as these are people who have spent most of their lives being or becoming good students who thereby pleased both their parents and teachers.

Clearly it is important that the therapist or counsellor is not intimidated by the cleverness that students might be determined to display. There is a need to respect their intelligence and abilities while at the same time avoiding the temptation to collude too far with the intellectually defensive strategy presented. Above all, therapists need to be able to counter the whole competitive, hierarchical set of values. It is much more likely that they will be able to do this if they are not themselves caught up in having to be 'experts' with special, and possibly arcane, knowledge. If they are unwilling to present themselves as ordinary human beings then they may not be able to demonstrate convincingly that one's fundamental value as a human being does not reside in having exceptional intellectual powers.

As I write this I am reminded again of parallels between Peter Lomas's views of therapy and Winnicott's thoughts about parent-child relationships. Both sorts of interaction are asymmetrical and in some sense non-reciprocal. They are also both destined – if all goes well – to be transcended or dissolved, as the child's dependency needs diminish or the therapy draws to a close. Most significantly, both share the somewhat paradoxical characteristic of being both ordinary and extraordinary.

Winnicott speaks of the 'Ordinary Devoted Mother' (1986, 3–14). He is at pains to emphasize that what the child needs is good-enough mothering, and that good-enough mothering is best done by mothers without interference from experts. What this ordinary devoted mother is expected to provide is everyday love, care and attention. Yet Winnicott's description of the infant–mother interaction makes it clear that it is also, in some ways, extraordinary. He views it as a highly intuitive attunement between newborn and carer that, over time, gradually lessens in intensity so that the baby is enabled to gain a sense of itself as a separate human being in relation to another.

There are, of course, significant differences between this and therapeutic interactions. The latter are not necessarily at all maternal or paternal. In fact Peter Lomas emphatically disagrees with Winnicott's view of therapy as a maternal space. He sees therapy as far more akin to friendship and not primarily as a developmental process. However much conscious and unconscious echoes from childhood are invoked, and however regressed clients may feel, they remain essentially adult and should be respected as such. Furthermore the therapist – however dedicated – is obviously not devoted to each client in quite the way parents are to their young children.

Despite this, the ordinary–extraordinary paradox of the mother–baby pair does have illuminating parallels with therapy. This latter may resemble other relationships in a person's life: parent, friend, mentor, but it is not the same as any of these. In fact, as already mentioned, some of its value rests in its being outside the person's usual life. Yet at the same time it is crucial that the special setting in which client and therapist meet does not tempt therapists to see *themselves* as either special or possessing extraordinary knowledge.

Jacques Lacan – an unlikely spokesman for the ordinary – has spoken of how the subject begins the analysis by speaking of himself without speaking to you or by speaking to you without speaking of himself. When he can speak to you of himself, the analysis will be completed.'[1] (Lacan, 1966: 373). It is hard to see how this shift can be accomplished if analysts and therapists hide behind their analytic masks and are not really there to be spoken to.

[1] I am grateful to John Forrester for this translation.

Chapter 5
The ordinary

JOHN M. HEATON

A central notion in the work of Peter Lomas is that of the 'ordinary'. He wrote a chapter called 'Ordinariness' (Lomas, 1994: 121–34) and much of his writing emphasizes the importance of the ordinary day-to-day experience of life and therapy. He also writes in ordinary language, eschewing arcane interpretations and explanations based on theoretical models, so showing the importance of ordinary language in enabling us to understand others and ourselves.

In this chapter I shall discuss the notion of the ordinary and its vital importance to psychotherapy in my own way, so hoping to deepen and expand Lomas's pioneering work.

The notion of 'ordinary' must be differentiated from notions like 'average', 'normal', 'typical', 'usual', and 'conventional'. All these words have a statistical ring, implying that there is a fixed, stable, constant and permanent given to its meaning. The 'ordinary', on the other hand, has no essence; it has no basic characteristic or formal structure that is common to a multiplicity of instances. Rather, the ordinary needs an enactment of thought to attain its meaning. It is more a way of being than a given, a possibility rather than a fixed actuality. Thus a New Guinea native can be living 'ordinarily' although to us he might appear extraordinary.

The ordinary implies something that is conformable to order or rule. It is derived from the Latin *ordinarius* – arranged in regular lines or courses. Now rules form a 'family' with no precisely delineated defining characteristic. The relation of rules to their use is such that not even the most precise formulation of a rule guarantees its flawless execution. Misunderstanding is always possible because the rule cannot compel compliance with itself. One learns how to follow rules by becoming habituated to certain reactions and procedures so that one can perform them automatically. Acting according to a rule is acting within a practice where significant regularity exists, and in which there is training and supervision, hence right and wrong ways of carrying on.

For example, to peruse the rules of tennis but never to have seen the game played or played it oneself, or seen a similar game played, would make the rules very difficult to interpret. One might wonder how high one could hit the ball for example. But once one has seen the game played, handled a tennis racket and so on, then its rules make sense. The rules are essential to the game and make sense but by themselves could be endlessly interpreted.

So the ordinary does not imply any standard outside of the particular way of life of the individual in his/her community. It is common sense and requires no interpretation from within the culture. 'It lies so artlessly before our eyes it is almost impossible to see' (Geertz, 1993: 92). Thus English people who shake hands on greeting one another require no interpretation of its meaning. But an anthropologist, someone strange to the culture, or a psychoanalyst who distances himself from his patient's culture, may wonder what is going on and may require an interpretation. The 'ordinary' points to what has to be accepted, the given, which serves as a pivot on which our lives turn.

'The fantastic and delirious pathos with which we have valorized the most exceptional acts has as its counterpart the absurd indifference and contempt in which we enshroud obscure and everyday actions. We are the dupes of rarity and we have thus depreciated even our daily bread' (Nietzsche, 1970: 353–4).

Ordinary language

Freud was the great pioneer in this century in developing a specialized language to describe and explain the psychological phenomena met with in everyday life and in the special circumstances of the consulting room. He thought that psychoanalysis was 'a procedure *sui generis,* something novel and special, which can only be understood with the help of new insights – or hypotheses, if that sounds better' (Freud, 1926: 186). By using the results of this procedure he thought he could generalize them so that they applied to everyday life and even to the nature of civilization and the past and future of religion.

He was troubled about the lack of authority and the variety of ordinary language in describing our mental life; he wanted a firm foundation upon which to build our knowledge of psychology.

> Have you not noticed that every philosopher, every imaginative writer, every historian and every biographer makes up his own psychology for himself, brings forward his own particular hypotheses concerning the interconnections and aims of mental acts – all more or less plausible and all equally untrustworthy? There is an evident lack of any common foundation. And it is for that reason too that in the field of psychology there is, so to speak, no respect and no authority. In that field everyone can 'run wild' as he chooses. If you raise a question in physics or chemistry, anyone who knows he possesses no 'technical knowledge' will hold his tongue. But if you venture

> upon a psychological assertion, you must be prepared to meet judgements and contradictions from every quarter. In this field, apparently, there is no 'technical knowledge'. Everyone has a mental life, so everyone regards himself as a psychologist. But that strikes me as an inadequate legal title. The story is told of how someone who applied for a post as a children's nurse was asked if she knew how to look after babies. 'Of course,' she replied, 'why, after all, I was once a baby myself'. (Freud ,1926: 187)

Every sentence of this quotation could be questioned. There is a lot to be said for the nurse's reply. If she was in touch with her experience as a baby this should be a good basis for looking after a baby herself. Most of us rightly hold our tongue about matters of physics and chemistry for the good reason that we have no experience of their objects and the investigations involved. But from birth onwards we are deeply involved in making psychological judgements. Does Mummy love me or not? How do I get Daddy's attention? Why does my big brother hit me at times? Most of our psychological judgements are true, otherwise ordinary life would be impossible. I can be perfectly clear that my wife is tired and does not want to listen to my moans about life, that someone does not like me, that I have made a stupid remark, that my friend is depressed, that we are all hungry, etc.

Of course we all make disastrous mistakes at times; the Sunday newspapers, films, novels, plays, are full of accounts of psychological misjudgements and lawyers depend on them to make a living. Some of us are better at making these judgements than others and most of us are probably just lucky that our disastrous misjudgements have not landed us on the front page of the newspapers or in a law court. We all know that in some areas of life, such as love, sex and religion, we can very easily go wrong and that dogmatism here is very unwise. And that familiarity is important as we can judge our friends and family better than we can judge strangers. But every adult is an expert at making psychological judgements, as we have had a long experience of doing so.

Freud complains that writers and historians make up their own psychology and have no common foundation. If this were really so we would have great difficulty in understanding them. Their foundation, however, is in the ordinary language of our common culture and human experience. As we have all had some experience of love, then, that is the foundation of our understanding of love stories. Of course we differ in the depth and subtlety of our understanding so that some of us are satisfied with pulp fiction whereas others can appreciate Stendhal and Sylvia Plath, but the basis of our understanding lies in our experience and our sensitivity to language.

As human beings can reflect on themselves and others, and as we have existed for thousands of years, we have evolved language to influence one another and to express our knowledge and confusions about others and ourselves. This is a vital part of ordinary language. Technical language, on the other hand, is evolved when we have to deal with an unfamiliar domain – the anatomy and physiology of the brain, subatomic particles and so on.

Careful attention to what people actually say to each other, the host of things we do in and by uttering words, the variety of infelicities and confusions to which they are subject, are the foundation on which any understanding of thought, feeling, action, and desire must be founded, for ordinary language is rich in subtle distinctions and has a huge range of idioms. It embodies the inherited experience and acumen of many generations. Ordinary language can be precise when used competently. The trouble is that the average person often uses it sloppily, hence one importance of literature where, at its best, it is used with sensitivity and precision.

What is it about human language that invites people, especially in the last hundred years or so, to repudiate its everyday use? What is the source of our desire for the technical? Why are we so captivated by 'ego', 'id', 'superego', 'internal object', 'mental process' and so on? Perhaps it is because they make us feel special and superior, that if we can use these words then that shows that we really understand the human mind. But these terms are actually very imprecise. For example, what precisely is a 'mental process'? The term 'ego' has many different meanings in the literature; thus some analysts want to strengthen it, others claim it is the source of all our troubles. Experienced analysts often disagree on what derives from the id or from the ego, or what the area of operation of the superego is. Metapsychological explanations such as the pleasure principle and reality principle refer to forces that are so undifferentiated that they are practically useless in clinical practice, where we are concerned with what patients actually say and do and how their words express their thoughts and feelings.

More importantly, talk of mental processes and mechanisms enables us to be morally neutral towards people, for mental processes are not people. So it enables us to treat people as if they were minds alone and control and 'cure' them in the way we think is best, reassuring ourselves that we are morally neutral. But a person is not a mind but an embodied being whom we treat as having responsibility, an ability to choose, an experience of freedom – in short, a moral being with rights and obligations. So persons are members of a group that provides the ambience in which meaningful discourse and rationality are possible and within which they live their lives.

Now we can be morally neutral towards objects and processes because they are not part of a rational community. But people are. Here we can try to be just and not swayed by our emotions but this is very different from being neutral. To be neutral to a person is morally monstrous as it denies his/her personhood, it shuts people out of the human community where moral language makes sense and it enables us to control them pretending it is for their good. It makes sense to do this to a body, as in much medicine, but a person is not just a body any more than just a mind. We can trust people and feel grateful or betrayed by them. Objects and processes can let us down – we like our cars and computers to be reliable and are upset if they let us down, but we do not feel that they can betray us. There is a big difference between a therapist who is reliable and one whom we can trust or who we feel has betrayed us.

If we are concerned about what people feel, desire, envy, think and so forth we should consider, amongst other things, in what sort of situations we should be willing to speak (or again be unwilling to speak) of somebody or ourselves feeling, wishing, wanting, envying, thinking, etc.

Thus what sorts of actions would lead us to apply or withhold the word 'abuse' without hesitation and when would we be unwilling or uncertain whether to apply or withhold this adjective? It is clear that if a person sincerely feels she has been abused then there can be no questioning the feeling provided we know she understands English and is not lying or play acting. It is important to see that the sentence 'I feel abused' makes sense but it is not, as such, a statement of knowledge. For knowledge is connected with doubt and certainty, with learning and finding out, with the possibility of mistake or deception, with grounds and confirmation. So I may truly feel abused but not know who has abused me, whether it is myself or someone else, and how and when. For bare feelings are incorrigible whereas knowledge has to be sought and can be questioned. To say 'I don't know whether I feel abused or not, maybe I do feel it, maybe I don't' is nonsense. But it does make sense to ask: 'who has abused me?' or 'what is the actual abuse and how do we define abuse?' or 'am I abusing myself?' Here we need grounds and confirmation, for we can be right or wrong about these matters.

A social worker told me that once he mentioned, at a meeting of social workers, that he had baths with his three-year-old daughter. He was severely reprimanded for this and told he was abusing her. This raises many questions. He told me that he was not doing anything sexual with her as far as he knew; his daughter seemed quite a healthy child and his wife did not see anything wrong in his having a bath with their daughter. It was convenient to give the child a bath when he had one. So how do we define abuse? Is the statement: 'a man having a bath with his three-year-old daughter is abusive' an analytic statement – a definition of abuse – or is it an empirical statement? If it is the latter then we can ask: how do we know whether the child felt abused or not? Assuming the man is telling the truth, on what grounds can we say he was abusing the child when he neither felt he was, nor was he doing anything sexual to her in his meaning of the word? Of course, we can resort to the unconscious and say he was unconsciously abusing her and that many years later the child would realize that she had been abused by her father –

especially if she underwent an appropriate form of psychotherapy. But then we are surreptitiously making abuse an analytic concept by changing its ordinary meaning and defining having a bath with one's three-year-old daughter as necessarily abusive.

But here we enter a tangle of confusions that I have not the space to undo (Bouveresse, 1995: 69–82). I can only say that to claim a child had been abused is an hypothesis that might be used to explain certain difficulties that brought her, when an adult, to psychotherapy. This hypothesis involves the notion of cause; it is assumed that the abuse caused the present troubles and has been acting all along but unconsciously. The investigation of causes, however, is meaningful only if it involves criteria for experimental verification. A cause is a fact that is independent of what it causes and the cause determines the effect. There may be contributing causes but these, too, are independent of what they effect.

But if a person 'now sees' that the cause of her unhappiness was the abuse, how can she know that this cause has been operative during the whole period in question, especially if it has been acting unconsciously? And how can the analyst know this, for, after all, there would have been innumerable causes acting on her besides the abuse? If it is claimed that the abuse was inscribed on a memory trace and so is causing the present misery then this assumption is based on a very dubious and unargued theory of memory – a theory that fails to recognize that memory is constructive and reconstructive rather than passively reproductive. All this assumes that she has been purely passive, subject to all the causes acting on her. But perhaps she has been abusing herself and if so bears some responsibility for this as she is doing it for a reason – a reason she may not be prepared to acknowledge, but a reason nevertheless. If we deny that she was responsible then we are denying her very humanity because human action, in contrast to what a computer can do, involves notions like responsibility, freedom, choice and reason.

The causal picture is an idealized, and vastly simplified, picture of persons, the way they live and how we praise and blame and attribute responsibility and reasons for their actions. Much of its seductiveness arises from the special language and the claims of scientific authority in which it is drawn.

The word 'abuse' has become a special word with a dogmatic use because of the confusions between the incorrigibility of the first person pronoun use: 'I feel abused' and its ordinary public and legal use: 'He is abusing'.

Conceptual matters must not be confused with empirical ones. If you are weeping and one asks: 'What makes you weep?' and you reply 'I'm terribly sad' then this is a conceptual matter and carries its own authority. It would be absurd to say to an adult in ordinary circumstances 'You are sad, that's why you weep'. Or 'How do you know that you are sad? Perhaps you are happy.' There can be no disagreement about one's own feeling in contrast to objective judgements where it makes sense to try to reach an agreement. We do not observe ourselves and so come to know that we are sad and not happy; however happy we look and behave we can always say that we are really sad. We can deceive ourselves and pretend we are happy but when this pretence is uncovered we then realize we are sad; it is not an empirical discovery. We can usually refrain from weeping when we are sad so in a sense we are responsible for weeping but this does not involve knowing that we are sad; sadness, like joy, envy, anger, despondency, is usually a response to a particular situation. In short, our feelings have their own authority. If I feel sad and speak fluent English, then no argument or demonstration need persuade me otherwise.

But empirical matters are very different, for here knowledge, proof, and error come into play. If I say I feel sad because my wife has just died it is always possible that I might be mistaken about the cause; perhaps she has not died after all or the person who told me mistook me for another. If I thought she had died then her supposed death would be the reason for my sadness.

Words like 'abuse' and 'persecution' need to be very carefully handled. Individuals may feel persecuted or abused and this feeling cannot be denied; but who is doing it, themselves or someone else or both? This requires evidence and proof and these are empirical matters that can be sorted out only by investigation.

The use and therefore the meaning of psychological words has to be attended to in order to see the particular situation that fits the suggested characterization. It is disastrous to allow oneself to be lured into the scientific model of explanation that favours generalization when specificity is required. We are then tempted to create a general characterization of an ordinary psychological word and so lose the ordinary use of the word that creates a meaning sensitive to context.

Expression

Freud neglects the expressivity of language – he fails to see the significance of the fact that every person expresses himself, his joys and sorrows, hates, fears, and despair, differently. It is how we express ourselves, the way we use language, that is significant and enables us to understand one another. There is a tremendous difference between a therapist who talks about loss and mourning because he has read about their importance in a book written in a scientific style, and a therapist who has experienced and struggled with them. They express themselves differently, there is a different resonance to their words, which is responded to by patients. It is the same with writers – each expresses himself or herself differently because a work of art conveys itself, not something else. This is why writers differ in their accounts of psychological life, not because they have no scientific basis for what they write, as

Freud thought. Writers do not convey feeling or thoughts in general and so do not write in an unexpressive scientific style; the difference in the way different writers express themselves is vital to our understanding and evaluation of them.

There is no standard way of expressing ourselves. We can only speak truly from where we are. That is the difference between expressing oneself and talking about things we have merely read when we merely cite a truth. The technical language of psychoanalysis and its exclusive claim to having the truth about conflict and mental pain covers over this essential difference. It tries to create a standard way of writing about human conflict at the cost of destroying the very spirit of human truth. It is the fact that there are these differences in expression that enables us to see that there is no literal or universal truth about human being.

Expression consists in its incalculability, and its infinite variations are an essential part of life. Thus a soulful facial expression is not describable in terms of the distribution of matter in space. A piece of music can be played with genuine expression in innumerable ways. The break up of psychoanalysis into so many different schools expresses a truth about the human condition that psychoanalysis seeks to repress.

Freud is worried about the lack of authority in writers and philosophers; they 'run wild', he claims. Does he really think that Sophocles, Shakespeare, Dante, Kant, Confucius and so on lack authority in their psychological insights? His idea of authority rests on uniformity. Freud and now the International Psychoanalytic Association and other lesser psychotherapeutic organizations have always tried to impose uniformity, each having its own idea of it. The result, of course, is the current chaos in the field of psychotherapy. Each 'authority', through various political and economic means, and its perversion of ordinary language, tries to impose its authority on as many people as possible. The careful weighing of evidence; the intimate relationship between words, concepts and practice; respect for differences of expression due to the differing experience of people; the vitality of the ordinary are all being ignored and suppressed.

The authority of great writers and thinkers derives from the power of their writing and the example of their lives. It is the power of their expression that conveys their vision, which enables us to see the authority of the truth they seek to convey. For the authority of truth can be conveyed only by someone who is already at home in it.

Explanation

An important source of the authority claimed by psychoanalysts and psychotherapists is that they, in contrast to ordinary people, have an explanation for human conflict. Lacan, for example, has an elaborate theory of aggressivity, relating it to tension of the narcissistic structure in the coming-into-being of the subject. In the course of his exposition he makes many acute observations of how aggression manifests in the psychoanalytic session. Slips of the tongue, hesitations, calculated absences, seductive advances, recriminations, reproaches, phantasmic fears, attempts at intimidation and so on are constantly observed in therapy as in everyday life – and are often hidden forms of aggression. The basic explanation for all this in psychoanalysis is in the notion of the death instinct.

One point against all this is to note that theory is not determined by data: a number of theories will explain any given body of data. So no one of them is implicit in the data. In psychotherapy, where the therapist is confronted with a vast number of data in even one session, to believe in any one explanatory theory is absurd. Some will retort that the theories in question uncover deep psychological reality, and hence there is a fact of the matter; the death instinct really does exist for example. But there is no evidence that the concept of the death instinct constitutes, or is readily transformable into, a satisfying analysis of the language and behaviour it purports to explain.

The question is whether these explanations have enabled anyone to be less aggressive. Lacan for a start seems to have been a pretty aggressive person (Roudinesco, 1997). Thus he had a sexual relationship with the daughter of a man in analysis with him, which resulted in this man committing suicide by shooting himself in the face (Roudinesco, 1997: 307). This would surely be a not unexpected result of Lacan's actions for many people who had never heard of Freud, let alone Lacan. Do we need to be analysts to see the aggression on both Lacan's and his patient's part? The history of psychoanalysis gives little evidence that psychoanalysts are less maliciously aggressive than the rest of mankind; they just have cleverer explanations for it as they consider themselves special 'professionals', above the ordinary.

What is vital in therapy is the ordinary meaning of words and this includes, of course, their reference. Thus a patient walked into my room and said, with a relaxed smile, that her last analyst told her she was very envious because of deprivation at her mother's breast. Not feeling much better from the explorations of this hypothesis, she said she wanted to try another school of therapy to find the real cause. Of course, it was not another school of therapy she needed but to see the nonsense and sheer effrontery of what she was saying.

If a person comes into a room and says with a smile that they have just swallowed a bottle of arsenic one would conclude that either they did not know the meaning of what they had said or were insane. It is much the same with envy, which is an immensely crippling emotion; so if one truly understood its meaning one would be unlikely to smile if one were envious. It is the response to these words that is vital to show the meaning. If one is reassuring and indicates that an inquiry into what caused the person to swallow arsenic or become envious is necessary, then this shows a deep misunderstanding of the words and situation.

Therapy needs to be a sobering experience rather than an exciting exploration of one's 'inner self' or other such fantasies. Most therapy, however, panders to people's vanity. Thus someone told me that he had had some 15 years of psychoanalysis from a top analyst and so he now knew the causes of most of his troubles and those of the human race. He was convinced of the truth of Freud's discoveries, which he claimed he had rediscovered for himself through his analysis. But he was as troubled as ever by his symptoms. Had he really attained self-knowledge?

Self-deception

The use of a special technical language in psychotherapy is one of the main sources of self-deception in the field of therapy. It gives the therapist an appearance of knowledge while covering over how he is deceiving himself.

Let us briefly look at Freud's self-analysis, which is the corner-stone of his theory and practice and which coincided with the very discovery of psychoanalysis itself. Now this self-analysis has been considered a heroic feat by Freud's hagiographers; it certainly made him special. I quote Ernest Jones:

> In the summer of 1897, the spell began to break and Freud undertook his most heroic feat – a psychoanalysis of his own unconscious. It is hard for us nowadays to imagine how momentous this achievement was, that difficulty being the fate of most pioneering exploits. Yet the uniqueness of the feat remains. Once done it is done forever. For no one again can be the first to explore those depths. (Jones, 1953: 319)

As Spence (1994: 97–117) has shown in detail, Freud's self-analysis has been surrounded with rhetoric and legend whereas little is known of what it actually consisted as Freud was very secretive about it. This, of course, is a well-known rhetorical device, for secrecy engenders curiosity and the belief that the person who holds the secret is someone special. The myth has provided psychoanalysis with an unassailable birthright and any criticism is quickly dismissed as ungrateful and probably envious, a failure to respect what it cost Freud in pain and suffering.

It is questionable how therapeutic Freud's self-analysis actually was. Before his analysis Freud was in the throes of a mid-life crisis (Anzieu, 1986: 562). He was gnawed by suffering and easily gave in to resentment, remorse, self-doubt and dependence on others. He was liable to depression and tended to wallow in failure. Seven years later he was more at ease with himself and his fear of death; phobias of taking trains or crossing the street had all eased but not disappeared. But perhaps this improvement was due to his getting over the mid-life crisis by natural means. After all, millions of ordinary folk get over this without any analysis whatever.

Freud's self-analysis was unique, but so was Augustine's and Montaigne's to mention only two famous and well-documented cases. It is sometimes claimed that Freud's self-analysis was unique because it involved a constant dialogue with his friend Fleiss. But Augustine and Montaigne both had close friends with whom they discussed their problems.

The main problem with Freud's self-analysis was that its chief aim was not self-knowledge but knowledge of psychical processes, which he thought would explain the problems he met with in his neurotic patients. He started off with certain assumptions about the nature of the mind and then proceeded to prove them; so much of his theory is a projection of his unacknowledged beliefs.

Psychoanalysis, he thought, was an instrument to obtain knowledge of the unconscious. So this knowledge became subordinate to the instrument; the field of knowledge was restricted to what is obtainable by means of the instrument. This then made self-knowledge a special field and so a special language was constructed by Freud to describe what he thought he had discovered. It never seems to have occurred to him that he was an inventor rather than a discoverer in that he created a system of notation that allowed him to redescribe our ordinary psychological language in terms of psychic processes and mental mechanisms.

Freud invented about 116 special notions during his self-analysis and these form the bedrock of all further work in psychoanalysis (Anzieu, 1986: 564). His inventive genius enabled him to produce long strings of formulae that explained what he thought he had discovered. For example, we have: dreams are wish fulfilments; perversions are the negative of neurosis; money is the symbolic equivalent of faeces; happiness is the achievement in maturity of a childhood wish; dreams are picture puzzles and also fulfilments of the wish to sleep; death wishes are directed against loved ones; threats of punishment for masturbation are the cause of pavor nocturnus and nightmares; unconscious motives determine morality, works of art, jokes and so on.

The trouble with all this is that it provided an answer only in theory. There is a deep dissociation between the reductive analysis of the theory, which seeks to explain phenomena, and the evidential value of our ordinary meaning judgements. Patients speak and act in ordinary language and it is this that enables them to make judgements, not Freud's special vocabulary.

Freud subtly distorted so as to psychologize; he transposed ordinary language into a specialized psychological language while giving the impression that the latter is more true because more scientific. Thus in discussing Oedipus in 1909 he tells us: 'The myth of King Oedipus, who killed his father and took his mother to wife, reveals, with little modification, the infantile wish.' In 1917 'The legend of Oedipus realizes, with only a slight softening, the two extreme wishes that arise from the son's situation – to kill his father and take his mother to wife.' These modifications and softenings are interpretations of the Sophoclean text (Genette, 1997: 324–7). The implicit rule that Freud obeys is to move from the apparently superficial text to the supposed deeper psychological explanation. Thus the proposition 'he thought he was killing his father out of self-interest or pride (a quarrel between an arrogant young man and an old man over the right of way at the cross-roads); in fact, he killed him out of jealousy' will be found more convincing if under Freud's spell than its opposite ('he believed himself to be in love with his mother and jealous of his father; in fact he was eyeing the throne'). For motives can be endlessly played with, especially if we ignore the occasions when it is appropriate to enquire about them, how we assesses them, and when enquiry about them is meaningless.

This substitution of motives, endlessly done by psychoanalysts, is a major procedure of semantic transformation. It is a literary device called transmotivation, which has been used by many writers and has been studied by Genette (1997). But Freud uses it as a move into a statement of a scientific truth. If we do not see this as merely a rhetorical flourish on Freud's part then we shall not listen to the evidential value of what is being said in ordinary language. So we lose touch with our ordinary judgements of motive and instead frame our judgements according to the theory we believe in.

For example, a patient who is English and a Christian and whom I had seen for two years or so sends me a Christmas card at Christmas. What should I do? What is her motive? Perhaps it is an expression of an infantile wish on the patient's part and so I should respond in the classical analytic manner and refuse the gift and interpret her action. Perhaps this would simply be mean on my part and be a manifestation of my anal-retentive wish for control over the patient. But on the other hand if I 'gave in' and accepted the card perhaps I am acting out of countertransference phantasies and surrendering to the patient's controlling projective identification.

There is no end to the motives one can impute to the therapist and the patient, but perhaps sending a card is an ordinary action for that patient and we do not seek motives for ordinary actions. It would be absurd to ask what is my motive for putting on my trousers when I get up in the morning but it might be worth enquiring why I took them off at a public meeting. Here again there is endless room for dispute. I say I took them off as a protest against bourgeois respectability; someone else might say it is because I am very narcissistic and will use every opportunity to show off. How do we assess these claims? Of course, if I said I took them off because the man in the moon told me to then this does not make ordinary sense.

People who have seen several therapists have often told me how each one takes exception to different aspects of the person's life and so will interpret motives accordingly. Some do not like signs of aggression, others have a fine eye for obsessional features, and others concentrate on sexual deviations, and so on. Thus one woman was married to a sexually inhibited man and during analysis started an affair. The analyst took exception to this and interpreted it as acting out of transference fantasies. Her second analyst on the other hand thought analysis had strengthened her ego's capacity for decision, which had accompanied the liberation of her sexuality, and so did not interpret her motives in terms of acting out. Neither therapist nor patient takes sufficient account of the depth of the motives that drive us to self-deception. And the therapist's moral stance is hidden behind his supposed scientific neutrality, special psychological language and his intonation – he will speak in a neutral tone of voice.

The demand that we understand ourselves entails the demand that we assess ourselves for self-deception. It is very easy to find instances of self-deception in our emotional life. That I believe I love X does not mean that she and others who know me are particularly convinced that I do, as attention to my words and actions may show. To say 'I love you' to someone requires full attention to understand its meaning. For not only are the words important but intonation, facial expression, gesture, occasion and the participants' understanding of these are all relevant. There is no rule to follow that spells out the meaning. To declare 'I love you' on a moonlit night in spring in the garden of a romantic hotel at the same time giving a diamond ring does not necessarily mean what it appears to say. Both parties can be profoundly deceived in this exchange, for we readily lie to ourselves as well as to others. What we think or believe is not necessarily true, however good the theory behind it.

The demand for an explanation for certain of our actions is dependent on what we are identified with. A married man having an affair and trying to bring it to an end may find himself wavering in the attempt. If he goes on seeing his lover at times but ends up with his wife he will see himself as having been rather weak and so he may feel that this weakness requires interpretation. If, on the other hand, he and his wife separate and he ends up living with his lover, then he will not see his infidelities as weak but as healthy and so they will not require interpretation. Thus there are no particular kinds of psychological event that require interpretation. The descriptions of what happened are available only retrospectively as part of an interpretation that establishes or re-establishes one's identifications (Williams. 1993: 44–6).

Freud thought that the concept of identification was not merely one psychical mechanism amongst others but the operation itself whereby the human subject is constituted. He thought the subject is the sum total of his or her identifications but that this totality is in no way a coherent relational system so there is conflict. He thus gave himself and his followers *carte blanche* to interpret everything. He did not understand that sane people are not identified with themselves or with anyone else. 'I am John Heaton' is not an identity statement. For an identity statement says that such and such an object is the same as such and such another object. But 'I' is not a referring term; it has important uses but these do not include naming or describing any object. 'John Heaton' refers to something but 'I' does not as 'I' is not a name and not an object.

I am aware of myself as myself without inferring this from any feature of myself. For even if I look for features of myself, for example by looking at myself in a mirror or thinking about myself, I am aware that it is I who am doing this. There is a 'spontaneity of thought' as Kant put it. Being myself is not a quality of me; not something others and I have in common. Awareness of myself as subject is awareness of myself as nothing more nor less than myself – as ordinary (Brook, 1994: 70–94). It is self-deception to think that the human subject is constituted by identifications; rather it is when we are neurotic that we so constitute ourselves and lose our spontaneity. This inevitably leads to conflict and thinking of ourselves as more or less than we are – as special.

Therapists are usually deeply identified with the way their particular school sees things, so they are self-deceived and have lost their spontaneity of thought. When this is so they will interpret the class of psychological events that is highlighted by their school as in need of interpretation. This hides the moralistic agenda of the founder of the school and his specialness, and inevitably leads to the conflicts between the schools of psychotherapy, each with its special psychological jargon, heroes and rivalries.

Asking ourselves whether we are self-deceived is an integral and natural part of evaluating whether we know ourselves. But logically we cannot accuse ourselves of self-deception in the present tense, for in the case of self-deception we cannot identify our own present self-deception. Here diagnosis is identical to cure. It makes no sense to say I am deceiving myself now in believing that I want a cup of tea. But later I may adopt a new perspective and see that I did not really want a cup of tea but needed an excuse to stop work. We can always develop a new perspective from which we can accuse our former selves of self-deception. Furthermore, if these earlier selves could speak they could accuse the new self of being self-deceived.

So there is no possible criterion by which we can determine that this is the perspective, this is the position from which I can see others and myself rightly. The possibility of self-deception is the device by which all final claims to self-knowledge can be undermined. This includes those claims that we have come to understand as the way we have deceived ourselves.

The attempt to search for an answer, to seek a remedy for self-deception, is to avoid the problem as the answer and the theory providing it become all-significant and not the problem. In self-deception we are the problem, not our unconscious, so the solution is not separate from the problem. The answer is in the problem, not away from it. If the answer is separate from the main issue then we create other problems – interminable analysis, for example, or knowing the answer in theory but still being in conflict.

It is freedom from the demand for an answer that is essential to the understanding of self-deception. This freedom gives the ease of full attention and the freedom to free associate. It is the right relationship to the problem that is essential rather than learning about mental processes, unconscious mechanisms and so on. The approach to the problem shapes the problem and decides its fate. As the problem is self-created there must be an end to self-deception. The person and his or her problems are one.

Psychotherapy seems to attract people for whom a single perspective has become authoritative. They do not see that they then become actors in a drama in which the main lines of the script have already been laid out. Often the drama is laid out in terms of the particular story of infantile development favoured by the school of therapy to which the therapist belongs; this gives it a scientific aura as being based on real processes. The root metaphors on which the story of development is built and the way they are culturally determined is rarely examined (Spence, 1994). Let alone whether a developmental model is necessarily the best basis for understanding psychotherapy. The real problem is how to understand and articulate the conflicts and tensions and find our place within them.

As Kant pointed out long ago all human knowing and understanding are rooted in space and time and our inner sense of the beings that we ourselves are, is rooted in time. Time is 'the form of inner sense, that is, of the intuition of ourselves and of our inner state' (Kant, 1929: B49, A33). So when we seek to understand ourselves, we are deceived if we fix ourselves in any theoretical position as time moves on and so a new interpretation is always possible.

But how do we orientate ourselves if all is in change and there are innumerable theoretical positions?

Orientation

Kant, in the *Critique of Pure Reason*, argued that, in physics and the other natural sciences, interpretation is primarily theoretical as it involves determinate judgement. But when we come to understand the cultural dimension of human life, and all psychotherapies in which change depends on a personal relationship come under this, then evaluation is involved and this must be derived from the transcendental conditions of reflective judgement.

Here theory is not foundational as in the natural sciences. For reflective judgement to be effective we need an orientation rooted in the feeling of life and a teleological orientation that makes sense of culture on the basis of common sense. It is here that the notion of the ordinary is crucial, for common sense and the ordinary are brothers. Common sense orientates the judgements of the individual to the community and provides the basis for what Kant calls an enlarged mode of thought – that is a thought that is not cramped and subjective, as occurs in neurosis (Kant, 1952: §20–22).

Common sense here does not mean the same as common opinion. For example, if my friends and I say it is common sense that Britain should join the European single currency, then this is merely a shared opinion. Common sense in Kant's meaning is more basic and the emphasis is on sense. Thus it is common sense that I am now sitting on a chair at a desk in a room; anyone in my culture would agree. If someone were to say: 'No, you are kneeling at an altar in a church' then, in ordinary circumstances, I would not know what he or she meant.

Without common sense we merely have a dyadic relation to other people. We understand them as orientated by their horizon or ours alone. So experience is seen as theory laden and context dependent. Theories are not grounded in any way and relativism prevails. Hence the huge number of theories in psychotherapy and the impossibility of reconciling them.

But when we see the relevance of common sense and our ordinary way of speaking and living we have a triadic relation with others. We are then orientated by the person before us and by our feeling of orientation towards the person as focused in us. We can then distinguish between ordinary judgements of experience, which are orientated by our theoretical framework, and immediate discriminatory judgements, which orientate us to our theoretical framework. This latter mode of orientation allows us to assert or dissent from what is commonly held. We can have our own standpoint but this is not in the air like so many theoretical positions in psychotherapy, for common sense relates us to all of humanity. Reflection to be sane must always refer back to our own self-understanding, which we embody in the way we live, and the ordinary mediates this (Makkreel, 1990). For common sense is 'the ordinary ability to keep ourselves from being imposed upon by gross contradictions, palpable inconsistencies, and unmask'd impostures' (Geertz, 1993: 93).

Peter Lomas's writing with its independence from received opinion in psychotherapy yet its originality and ordinariness illustrate, I think, the truth of Kant's thesis, which itself, however, is written in a somewhat extraordinary manner.

Chapter 6
Imagination and metaphor in the development of the trainee psychotherapist

ROSEMARY RANDALL.

What qualities are looked for in the trainee psychotherapist? In her guide to psychotherapy trainings, Jan Abram (Abram, 1992) asked training organizations for their selection criteria. Their responses are rather bland and range from the strictly academic to the cautiously personal. At the academic end are the familiar requests for degrees. At the personal end qualities such as maturity, self-reflection and emotional capacity are suggested. The prospective trainee might be forgiven for finding this a little dull.

Peter Lomas, while acknowledging the difficulty of defining what might be required, is more explicit. He writes of vocation, of wisdom (the capacity for judging rightly in matters of life and conduct), of intuition and of the qualities required in ordinary living: 'strength, honesty, patience, humility, humour, shrewdness, a capacity to love, and so on' (Lomas, 1994: 9).

Nina Coltart agrees about vocation. She believes that it is made up of five features: 'giftedness, belief in the power of the unconscious, (indeed in the unconscious itself), strength of purpose, reparativeness and curiosity' (Coltart, 1996: 34). She also agrees about the difficulty of defining what is essential: 'Giftedness is easier to recognise than to describe...the gifted person brings to the work, creativity, imagination, adventurousness, curiosity, a strong reparative drive and...an ingredient x, which permeates the whole' (Coltart, 1996: 36).

In another context, Christopher Bollas celebrates the importance of the therapist's multi-faceted personality: 'analysands . . . use the different parts of the analyst's personality. They use the analyst's thoughtfulness, humour, sensuality, doubt, aggression, language capacity, memory, critical-interpretive ability, phantasy life, uninterpretiveness, maternal holding function, paternal presence – a list of personality elements that is virtually endless' (Bollas, 1989:101).

All three writers agree on the importance of something in the therapist that is unique and personal, hard to define but essential to the work.

Christopher Bollas speaks of the importance of 'idiom', a concept he acknowledges is close to Winnicott's 'true self'. Peter Lomas uses the more ordinary term 'voice' and the idea of personal style: 'a good training is one which allows and encourages students to trust, as far as possible, their own intuitive capacity, and to build on their own style of being with people rather than suppressing it and replacing it with a formula for behaviour imposed from without' (Lomas, 1994: 137).

I would like to argue for the importance of imagination in the voice, idiom or personal style of the developing therapist and for the role of metaphor in sustaining and cultivating it. By imagination I mean a quality that is close to empathy but goes beyond it. Imagination speaks of what is done with an understanding, what is made of it in the relationship between therapist and patient. It speaks of the opening up, deepening and developing of intuitive insight. It is a quality that draws on the unconscious and on dreaming. It can live in a moment of reverie or spontaneous playfulness and die momentarily from a destructive attack. Too often it may simply lie blunted and useless beneath the remorseless use of falsely premised reason or the obsessional enumeration of disconnected fact.

Coleridge's distinctions between fancy and imagination may be helpful here. For Coleridge, fancy is a lesser faculty, restricted to description and reproduction. It is 'a mode of memory' and 'has no other counters to play with but fixities and definites' (Coleridge, 1817: 167). It can mirror, copy, describe and re-arrange, but stops short of the imagination Coleridge believed essential to poetry and which may be essential to psychotherapy too.

Imagination, in contrast, is a transforming, energetic, creative force. It is the 'modifying and co-adunating Faculty' whose function is to 'send ourselves out of ourselves, to think ourselves in to the Thoughts and Feelings of Beings in circumstances wholly and strangely different from our own.' (Coleridge, letters to Sotheby, quoted in Holmes 1989: 326). It is 'the living power and prime agent of all human perception...It dissolves, diffuses, dissipates, in order to re-create; . . . it is essentially vital . . . ' (Coleridge, 1817: 167).

Co-adunating – meaning an action of joining together – is a term taken from biology and, as M H Abrams (1953) points out, Coleridge's dominant metaphor for the imagination is the growth of living things. Living imagination is counterposed to mechanical fancy. Where fancy copies, imagination imitates and develops. If fancy mirrors, imagination will create a new light. Coleridge's definition emphasizes both the empathic and transforming aspects of imagination and suggests that it has both conscious and unconscious dimensions. (See Rycroft, 1968 and 1985 for a more detailed discussion of the relation of Coleridge's thought to psychoanalysis.)

Coleridge's imagination is solitary, focused on poetic creation. It works on the world as its material to produce the new – the poem – that

Imagination and metaphor 81

will then be read and transformed in the mind of the other. The psychotherapist's use of imagination must of necessity be reciprocal. It operates in a shared space, acting and re-acting with the imagination of the patient to transform and heal.

The point at which the imaginative response develops out of the purely empathic one is often fed by metaphor, offered sometimes by the patient, sometimes by the therapist. The pleasure of the metaphor lies in its capacity to handle paradox and ambiguity, to free an unconscious thought, to offer approximation, possibility and development. Here are two examples from today's work.

G says (with distaste, talking of a situation at work): 'It would be special pleading. I'd be like a puppy, fawning.'

The image both defines and subverts. G is not a puppy, but like a puppy. The puppy, I imagine, will not be the puppy he imagines but in its simultaneous affinity and difference, connection and communication open up. I picture briefly my own childhood dog racing along a beach, barking at seagulls. I wonder which of the dogs of his childhood he has in mind and am lost for a moment in connection to the many stories he has told of his family's dogs and his frequent identifications with them. I see for a moment a puppy in the room with us eagerly pushing its head up against his hand and have a sense of G's potential mastery and confidence, which, in the story he is telling, he is uneasy about and hesitant to exercise. I do not reply directly to the image but its reverberations work their way into my responses.

The second example is from D, a young man who has been deeply depressed and who can find little in life to be hopeful about. The conversation takes place about 40 minutes into a difficult session in which he has talked despairingly of his hopelessness about therapy:

Me: You long for me to give you an answer like a doctor giving medicine [his image from earlier in the session] but you've also told me how much you hated the way your parents always seemed to prescribe things to you. It's very hard for you to find a way of taking or receiving anything that feels OK.

D: [bad-temperedly] You give me a paradox. It's not helpful. What am I supposed to do?

Me: You feel I'm like a Zen master?

D collapses in giggles. The image is deeply incongruous and funny to him. We talk about what it means to him and I say a little of the image that was in my mind when I spoke. He pictured a little old man on a mountainside, talking gibberish, ludicrous and ridiculous. I was thinking of the Zen master who hits the novice regardless of what he says. Both images carry great hostility and I think it is this that has been articulated and released through the metaphor. The atmosphere in the room lightens a little. I feel a little more connection with D and we are able to continue talking although, as often, we slide more and more towards the abstract. A few minutes later I say:

Me: Perhaps you think a feeling can't go anywhere?

D: What do you mean?

Me: Have an effect – an outcome . . .

D: That doesn't make sense. Feelings aren't like that. (Pause) They're just there. Like the weather.

This metaphor helps us find a way of talking about the disconnection and the way feelings seem to D to arrive from nowhere. They simply exist around him, outside his control, unpredictable, unforecastable, and uninfluenceable. I also have a feeling of reciprocity. I offered a metaphor that was an opening. He offered one in return.

This way of thinking and playing with an image or metaphor is a familiar part of psychotherapeutic work. Aspects of it can be talked of in other terms, for example as free association or counter-transference. I prefer to think of it as imagination because this emphasizes both the conscious and unconscious aspects, and the empathic and creative qualities. It is a state that is dipped in and out of in the course of a session, some of its associations offered in response, some rejected, some simply left to form part of a shared, unconscious communication. It is also a highly individual state. Each psychotherapist uses it differently and it changes with each patient. Each trainee has to find his or her own way of developing it as part of their own individual style.

In the literature, psychotherapy often expresses itself most eloquently through its metaphors. There are metaphors for the process itself. Therapy is a story, a drama, a journey, an archaeological excavation. There are metaphors for relationships of all kinds – Oedipus, narcissus, the baby at the breast, the mother and child – and metaphors for the mind – topographical, energetic, communicative, idiomatic. Writers sometimes reveal themselves most personally through their choice of metaphor. Freud, for example, in his case-study of 'Dora' (Freud, 1905b: Vol. VII) is successively archaeologist, geographer, marksman, wrestler with demons, locksmith and deaf man. Most famously in his letter to Fliess about the case, he is a thief – an image which captures both his pride and satisfaction in his skill and his misappropriation of another's secrets: 'It has been a lively time and has brought a new patient, an eighteen year old girl, a case that has smoothly opened to the existing collection of picklocks' (Freud, in Masson, 1985: 427).

Metaphor creates a potential space, a moment for imagining where, despite the apparent clarity of the image, an alternative or opposite view can emerge. There is room for uncertainty and interpretation. Dissonance and ambiguity can give way to a shared insight or create a new perspective. Ignês Sodré and A S Byatt capture the fruitfulness and importance of this uncertainty well in their discussions on psychoanalysis and literature. They compare the sharing of dreams and stories and the kind of communication that takes place:

> Byatt: We do have to feel it as well. You wrote, in your article about dreaming, that a dream-image wolf in an analysis is an image which exists as a dream image, a picture you said, in the mind of the patient, and is then offered by the patient to the analyst who, if he or she is listening properly, makes her own or his own picture, which is not the same, and yet these two pictures must communicate. This reminded me of things I've written in my own novels again and again and again, of a kind of image hovering between two people, shared, as you always share somebody's image if you read properly, but you know you're not visualising the same scene. (Byatt and Sodré, 1995: 239)

Byatt then talks of how she gradually learnt as a novelist to allow this space existence in her writing:

> Byatt: When I was a young novelist, I always told everybody too much because I was so excited by the richness of what I could see. If I did visualise a room I could see every little thing in it glittering and glittering and I wanted to share the whole thing. An editor once said to me about another novelist: 'she leaves no room for other people's imagination' and I suddenly realised she was actually saying it to me about me and that there are places where you must leave a space. (Byatt and Sodré, 1995: 240)

Byatt's phrase in the first quotation 'a kind of image hovering between two people' is a possibly unconscious reference to a phrase of Coleridge's in his lectures on Shakespeare where he speaks of 'a middle state of mind more strictly appropriate to the imagination than any other when it is hovering between two images' (Coleridge, 1811: 311). Although planned, the conversations with Sodré took place unscripted. As a literary scholar as well as a novelist, Byatt would be likely to be familiar with Coleridge's lectures and the echo of his phrase in her own thus seems a happy example of the way in which imagination works unconsciously, connecting and deepening an insight without necessarily provoking or requiring reference. Byatt has made it her own, although the connection to Coleridge remains.

Metaphor is one way of opening up an imaginative space but of course is not the only way. There are many aspects of language and style that may contribute. For example, Winnicott is more inclined to present a paradox, a piece of understatement or a snatch of clinical material that is left hanging and suggestive. Searles creates space by the use of generous, explanatory prose aimed always at communicative accuracy. Balint swoops and dives with extended enthusiasms, rests soberly in detailed, thoughtful explanation and then sweeps off again, giving an enchanting quality to some of his writing. Peter Lomas roots himself in the ordinary. His metaphors are everyday ones and his language is direct. These writers each have their own individual way of creating a space for the reader – a space that they can use or refuse, embrace or reject. They are all writers who offer themselves openly, who give the sense that to read them might be rather like meeting them. The reader, too, must arrive with imagination, a willingness for excitement, receptiveness or reverie and the courage for strong feeling. Where a writer is less gifted, more guarded or given to artifice and conceit, the space may feel smaller or cluttered or confused. The reader's imagination must work correspondingly harder but the process is essentially the same.

Respect for a shared imaginative space is not valued by all analytic writers. Donald Spence in his controversial book *Narrative Truth and Historical Truth* (Spence, 1982) laments the impossibility of knowing exactly what the patient visualizes in a dream and excoriates the profession for its lack of prompt, exact and scientific recording and reporting of the detail of sessions. Where Byatt and Sodré celebrate the impossibility of exactitude, Spence abhors it. Reflecting, as do Sodré and Byatt, on the analogous relationships of therapist and patient, reader and writer, Spence says disappointedly: '...because there is no one-to-one correspondence between text and reality the reader can never be sure of exactly reversing the transformation produced by the author' (Spence, 1982: 51). His wish is for an exact replication of the patient's perceptions in the mind of the therapist. He longs to be sure that both are looking at exactly the same thing. Coleridge refers to this empiricist privileging of the visual as a 'despotism of the eye' (Coleridge, 1817: 62) Over-valuing of scientific, observational scrutiny leads, I think, to the death of the open, shared, imaginative and communicative space that is at the heart of a psychotherapeutic endeavour. The ideology of such a position is betrayed in Spence's own language and use of metaphor. He scarcely mentions the relationship of patient and therapist. His images are of 'data', 'phenomena', 'checking', 'goals' and 'targets'. The analyst is active and investigative. The patient is his passive material whose halting productions are compared unfavourably to the work of a bad novelist.

This tension between the wish to be part of an empirical science and the need to inhabit the realm of imagination and ambiguity has dogged psychoanalysis since Freud and is perhaps responsible for the tendency in psychoanalysis to kill off it best metaphors, reifying them, explaining them and fixing them until they are as dead as the mouth of the river and the foot of the mountain that so many of my generation learnt about in school.

When Freud wrote to Fliess in October 1897 that 'Everyone was once a budding Oedipus in fantasy' (Freud, in Masson, 1985: 272) he offered a metaphor with multiple reference points for the thoughtful reader. We do not know what Fliess made of it (except that he did not reply very promptly, for Freud asks him three weeks later to respond) but it was open to him to imagine any part of the myth and to form his own associations and interpretations. He might, like Freud, have dwelt on Oedipus's desire for his mother. But he might also have wondered about Jocasta and Laius's treatment of their infant son, about Jocasta's self-deception, about Oedipus's desire to know himself, about the play's themes of revenge and violence and its pessimistic view of human happiness. Such possibilities remain open in *The Interpretation of Dreams*, where Freud writes with tolerant humour: 'Being in love with the one parent and hating the other are among the essential constituents of the stock of psychical impulses' (Freud, 1900: Vol. IV: 261) and:

> Today, just as then, many men dream of having sexual relations with their mothers, and speak of the fact with indignation and astonishment. It is clearly the key to the tragedy and the complement to the dream of the dreamer's father being dead. The story of Oedipus is the reaction of the imagination to these two typical dreams. (Freud, 1900: 264).

But by 1923 when Freud published *The Ego and the Id*, Sophocles is largely forgotten and Freud's own language and presentation of the matter has changed. He is dry, definite and exact. Oedipus is no longer metaphor but scientific fact. He writes, for example:

> At the dissolution of the Oedipus complex the four trends of which it consists will group themselves in such a way as to produce a father-identification and a mother-identification. The father identification will preserve the object-relation to the mother which belonged to the positive complex and will at the same time replace the object relation to the father which belonged to the inverted complex: and the same will be true mutatis mutandis, of the mother identification' (Freud, 1923: Vol. XIX: 34).

And so on. It would be wrong to say that nothing is gained in all this but something is lost. Oedipus is no longer available as shared myth and metaphor, only as complex, symptom, diagnosis.

M told me with some anxiety that she could tell me no coherent story of her life. In particular she could make little sense of her early childhood. She wanted to be able to tell such a story. She had read in a popular magazine that it was a sign of mental health to be able to offer a coherent narrative of this kind. (The article she read seems to have been based on the work of attachment theorists who have found a strong correlation between secure attachment and coherent autobiographical stories (see for example Main, 1991, or the summary in Holmes, 1993.) She had gathered from this that no matter how difficult the life events you described, if you could understand them in narrative form you would somehow be all right. Her lack of a story confronted her as a terrifying emptiness, a confirmation of desperate chaos but the idea of the story that might contain it or fill it carried no hope. This was not story as metaphor that could be explored and inhabited, its limits pressed and the difference between life and story eventually enjoyed. She experienced her lack of a story as a symptom and offered it to me as such – frightening, solid and unapproachable. She could do nothing with it except simultaneously fear it and hold on to it. What she demonstrated was the fate of metaphor when it is theorized. It loses its ambiguity, its paradox, its sinuous responsiveness and individual plasticity. It dies and is henceforth of little imaginative use.

Psychotherapy trainees are usually expected to read widely in psychoanalytic literature and they daily encounter the views of others in supervisions, classes and discussions with peers and colleagues. Contradictory views, incompatible theories, arcane and idiosyncratic expositions are inevitably a part of this (as are hopefully, lucid and entertaining explanations, supportive criticism and a sense of a delightful and varied literature.) It can be a baffling and difficult environment in which to develop a truly personal sense of voice. Too often imagination seems to be left behind and a conventional, academic understanding substituted. Sometimes the trainee's voice can seem dead, crushed or nonexistent, perhaps where there has been an over-enthusiastic embrace of theoretical understanding or a compliant deference to the views of others. More often there can be a sense of unprocessed connections and allegiances, sometimes to people and sometimes to theories. Occasionally one meets someone who seems to have sailed through untouched but whose 'voice' is the unsubtle clangour of the unresisted 'I' rather than the subversive, surprising tones of the truly individual subject.

Too often, psychotherapy trainings seem to accept as inevitable some crushing of the spirit, as if the fear that someone might come through untouched leads to an insistence on conformity, rigour, monitoring and demonstration of competence. Nina Coltart, who in other respects is an enlightened and illuminating commentator on the repressive effects of training, none the less contends that an exciting, mutually enriching relationship is not to be expected with a supervisee in training. In an essay that celebrates a free and invigorating supervisory relationship with a junior colleague she writes:

> It is certainly true that during the training the supervisor is inevitably experienced by the student as being – and simply is – in a dominant position of

authority; a lot of straight teaching has to be done, and furthermore, both participants know that reports are written throughout, and that they finally weigh heavily in the assessment for qualification. (Coltart, 1996: 116)

Training is seen a rite of passage and only after it is completed can truly creative thought in a pleasurable relationship be contemplated.

A training, like that of the Cambridge Society for Psychotherapy, which tries to remove such restraints, may get rid of external inhibitions but leaves the trainee just as subject to internal restrictions. When I was an undergraduate I read Freud's *The Interpretation of Dreams* and was excited and amazed. A few years later someone gave me a paper of Winnicott's that made me cry. Yet as a psychotherapy trainee I initially read the literature either with an academic determination or not at all. I lost the freedom to react imaginatively in both an intellectual and an emotional sense. I compared one theory with another, critically measuring each against each. I tried to apply them to my clinical work and to match this experience with what I was reading. I worried over how to convey theoretical insights to patients. I felt sterile and lost. So I'd quit for a while, read nothing for months but novels and drift along with my patients in a different, more comfortable space but one that lacked bite. I'd return to the literature seeking stimulation and a sharper edge to my thoughts. Gradually I recovered the capacity simply to read for pleasure, with emotional responsiveness and imagination, and to trust that an unconscious as well as a conscious integration might take place. These inhibitions were my own but I do not think I was the only trainee to experience such dilemmas. They are inherent in the tension in the literature between science and hermeneutics. They draw weight from the individual's previous educational experiences. They are coloured by transferences to therapist, supervisors, institutions and colleagues. There may be difficulty, too, in the experience of reading about oneself that the literature can present. There can be moments in therapy when the literature is too painful to read openly and is better left to one side if intellectual defences and imaginative inhibitions are not to be encouraged.

Winnicott talks of the way the baby makes the world anew, inventing it as it were for itself. Of course it is, in fact, a shared world, a world that is discovered, a very old world in some senses, full of the repetitions of generations. Winnicott stresses the importance of the moment of illusion. Out of this develops the possibility of transitional space and creativity: 'the baby creates the object, but the object was there waiting to be created and to become a cathected object' (Winnicott, 1971: 104).

'As observers we note that everything in the play has been done before, has been felt before, has been smelt before . . . Yet for the baby (if the mother can supply the right conditions) every detail of the baby's life is an example of creative living' (Winnicott, 1971: 119).

Here is a possible metaphor for the way in which each individual must find his or her own voice, the language and metaphor that will be personal to them but drawn from the collective inheritance and culture, transformed by the way they live it and communicate it to others.

Winnicott also distinguishes between imagination and fantasy. This is a slightly different distinction from Coleridge's and useful in a different way. Fantasy is the dead, static, repetitious space where 'what happens happens immediately, except that it does not happen at all' (Winnicott, 1971: 32).

For Winnicott, 'fantasying interferes with action and with life in the real or external world, but much more so it interferes with dream and with the personal or inner psychic reality, the living core of the individual personality' (Winnicott, 1971: 37).

If the literature is approached in a dissociated, academic manner, the kind of fantasizing that results is likely to be coloured by certainty and aggression. If it is read with compliance the fantasying may be more anxious and uncertain, whereas if the literature is ignored (or perhaps attacked in an anti-intellectual way) then the trainee may remain in an illusory and omnipotent state of great fragility.

What then must the psychotherapy trainee do in order to engage with imagination rather than with fantasy or dissociation? The task, as I have suggested, is made difficult by the tendency within psychoanalytic literature to deny or undermine its imaginative inheritance or treat it with ambivalence. It is complicated by traditional teaching attitudes that demand the absorption of large amounts of information in a set order, and may encourage caution or deference from novices. (People often seem to be told that they should learn to walk before they run, but have you ever watched what babies do when they first get on their feet? They launch themselves precipitously into space, lurching, staggering, running and flying but definitely not walking. That is a sober activity that comes later, if at all.)

What is required is an inner act of freedom that allows the trainee to respond with an excitement that is both emotional and intellectual, to connect not by applying insights from theory to practice or through translating from clinical work to the literature, but through living and dreaming in both. They may be rebellious, accepting, critical or conventional, but if they have been able to make something their own with courage and imagination they may be of some use in the work and enjoy it.

Chapter 7
Peter Lomas: friend and fellow writer

DAVID HOLBROOK

I ought to make it clear from the start that I write about Peter Lomas as a friend and fellow author: I am neither a colleague in the therapy business nor a sometime patient. I have consulted him professionally on at least one occasion, when I was experiencing personal difficulties with which I found it hard to cope by myself, but I have not had a course of psychotherapy with him; and so I cannot write of his psychotherapeutic work from personal experience. I have, it is true, written about psychotherapy 'from the outside', as it seemed to me, in its theory, to offer valuable insights into human nature and conflict – but I was urged by no less a person than D W Winnicott to remain 'outside', if I could, as one who considered and invoked claims from psychotherapeutic sources, in literary criticism and other forms of discourse. Meanwhile, my wife and I have maintained close relationship with Peter, and have exchanged with him considerations of authorship. So, I write about him as an author with whom I share a view of the nature and importance of the inward life, with a surprising degree of recognition of acquaintance with authors who have written about this problem, from Winnicott to Marjorie Grene, and from Ian D Suttie to Irving Yalom. I was glad to have the opportunity to write about his published work, as my regard for his writings has deepened over the years.

It has always been a comfort to know that there was such a practitioner in the neighbourhood. The mere existence of his wisdom in the background, should ever we need help, seemed enough to enable one to bear the more disturbed moments in one's life, and by degrees, I suppose, we became able to deal with our problems, by the distant proxy shadow of a psychic helper – a role of which the psychotherapist himself is probably unaware.

What strikes the reader most about the writings of Peter Lomas is their plain spokenness, which is not a mere matter of vocabulary:

> If the arguments of this book appear rather obvious to some readers, I would ask them to look at it as a record of my attempts to escape from the obscurities of a speciality into the common light of day. And if the language that I use is simple, this is not out of a desire to avoid complexity, but because I believe that ordinary language is the most adequate means available to convey the facts of human experience. (Lomas, 1973: 19)

To resist the customary assumptions about 'illness', especially mental illness, makes for an approach that many find irritating, if not maddening, and no doubt this is the effect Peter Lomas's writing has on some people. But after cool and careful reflection on his writing this hesitancy can be welcomed as an eye-opener. Indeed, it can be seen as the manifestation of an unusual spirit and a disturbing honesty. At least the man is always present: one can always hear his voice, hesitant, tentative, qualifying, even apologetic and at times confessional, and this deflates any tendency to elevate the writer into a god-like, all-seeing, idealized guru, which is no doubt the author's intention.

What is startling about Peter Lomas's writing about his psychotherapeutic practice is its direct and honest straightforwardness. After quoting the comments of a withdrawn, lonely and hopeless patient (Lomas, 1973: 13), he declares 'They are concerned with love'. This preoccupation is sustained throughout his writings. At the centre of all his work is this attention to the need for love:

> The patients are bringing to me, of their own volition, basic problems of living: first and foremost, of love; and I am trying to understand and to help them. In doing so I bring to bear (implicitly or explicitly) my own philosophy of living... (Lomas, 1973: 14)

The general impression given by his writing is one of uncommon honesty:

> A rather different reason for the psychotherapist's reluctance to describe his work in ordinary terms is a kind of shyness... The psychotherapist avoids it [i.e. the problem of seeming immodest – D H] by saying "not I but the technique..."

With him it is his very unwillingness to set himself up as any kind of superior being which generates his books – though we know them to be by a successful and long-established therapist:

> One is up against the kind of problems which make true autobiographies so difficult to write... Even when I am prepared to reveal all that went on I might still require the genius of a Tolstoy if I am to do justice in print to the subtleties of the encounter... (Lomas, 1973: 136)

So, one is left with the question: 'why should these qualities of the therapist be more effective in helping the patient than those of his friends and relations?' He answers this question thus:

> Firstly, the therapist is placed in a position calculated to evoke the best in him. A need for help has been identified . . . In a potentially fruitful therapeutic situation the patient has asked for help and the therapist is not encumbered by involvement in a confusion or power-struggle of long standing. He accepts psychological illness as an ordinary fact of life and in doing this he often supplies an environment which has been denied to the sick person. He is not dismayed or guilty or affronted or ashamed if his patient is ill – as a close relative may be. He is given, again in potentially fruitful encounters, the time and the freedom from extraneous interruption, and demands to devote himself to the patient and his problems . . .
> Secondly, the therapist is experienced in treating sick people. He has learned something of the way in which human anguish manifests itself and the sort of response that is need to help. He is accustomed to looking for the truth that is concealed . . . (Lomas, 1973: 136–7)

The difficulty Lomas faces is that today 'the whole climate of opinion that has grown from Freud tends to inhibit emotional reciprocity in the warmest of therapists' (Lomas, 1973: 139).

In many of his accounts Lomas reveals that he himself broke out of this pattern, allowing himself to respond to patients in ways that were unconventional, and which he would be hard put to explain along conventional lines. For example, he gives an extraordinary account of therapy with a woman who needed him to talk about himself, while she held on to him:

> I find it difficult to formulate what was happening between us in terms of a psychotherapeutic procedure . . . she was unconsciously manoeuvring me to repeat her mother's failure of handling her when she was a baby – yet desperately needing me to avoid these failures . . . (Lomas, 1973: 145)

He explains his response thus: 'Natural responses, as occur in ordinary life, are sometimes of crucial importance in therapy . . .' (Lomas, 1973: 146).

And, as one judges from his writings, he has gradually learned, but only painfully, to relinquish a studied, distant manner, imposed by the generally accepted conventions of psychoanalysis, for a more spontaneous, and sometimes quite unorthodox manner.

Thus, reading Peter Lomas is to experience a continual process of self-examination. He is extraordinarily unwilling to let anything pass:

> It is, in fact, appallingly difficult to communicate usefully about therapy; first, because there is no generally acceptable definition of health (and therefore of cure); and, secondly, because those who are anxious to bring about a beneficial change in people's their lives are, through human frailty, liable to

overvalue their method and results. Moreover, therapy can be adequately demonstrated only in cases where accurate diagnosis has been made. ('The Study of Family Relations' in Lomas, 1967a: 24)

At the same time he is also unorthodox in recommending what to some must seem outrageous, as when he quotes Hobson, who

recommends the study of Shakespeare and the Authorized Version of the Bible, and, indeed, he is the only therapist who believes that poets and novelists have more to teach about the nature of relationships than does psychology, let alone medicine. (Lomas, 1994: 136)

In general, Peter Lomas is a great demystifier:

The need now, I believe, is to demystify the practice of psychotherapy and to recognise that the experiences within it are not only part of the natural world but can be encompassed by our ordinary capacities for experience . . . (Lomas, 1994: 134)

He asks questions that other writers take for granted ('What is illness?' Lomas, 1973: 23). He even dares to question the common assumptions of his profession: 'Why should these qualities of the therapist be more effective in helping the patient than those of his friends and relatives?' (Lomas, 1973: 136)

He answers this by making somewhat modest claims. First, that 'the therapist is not encumbered by involvement in the confusion of power struggles of long standing'. He has the capacity to focus on the patient. Secondly, he brings his experience to bear, 'having learned something of the way in which human anguish manifests itself over the sort of response that is need to help'.

By page 147 of this book of 150 pages, Peter Lomas can afford to ask 'What, then, is psychotherapy?' He answers, surprisingly, by asserting that 'psychotherapy is an ordinary interpersonal activity' of a kind that 'would be taken for granted by a healthy society'. Not that it is painless. But he reiterates his belief that 'love helps patients', albeit making it clear that this is not a sentimental attitude from which 'all iron has been extracted' (Lomas, 1973: 150). 'What I am trying to show is that psychotherapy is primarily an ordinary interpersonal activity' (Lomas, 1973: 149).

The Case for a Personal Psychotherapy (1981) seems to have been written at a time when the intellectual climate was bedevilled by an outburst of false influences and doubtful movements, and this no doubt brought its pressure to bear on Peter Lomas's natural tentative manner of expression. He registers time and again his hesitancy, in trying to find the right means, the right voice in which to address his public:

> In seeking for an ordinary way of describing psychotherapy we are faced, time and again, with the problem of finding our way between the 'hard', obsessionally neat formulations of the scientist and the 'soft', flowery words of those who write about their work with naive sentimentality. The task is comparable to that of writing good poetry. The man-in-the-street may be moved by a sunset as deeply as the poet but if he tries to describe his emotions he will likely utter banalities. The psychotherapist who attempts to convey the significant experience in his work will almost certainly lack the necessary poetic gift, yet he can no more improve his communication by resorting to special language than can the poet. He can only write as clearly and truthfully as possible, recognizing that to take cover behind the aridity of the conventional, objective 'case history' may ensure professional respectability but lead him into the fatal error described by Blake:
>
> He who bends to himself a joy
> May the winged life destroy...
>
> (Lomas, 1981: 110–11)

There is also the danger of distorting the total communication by special techniques which inhibit communication: Lomas believes that this kind of error can be avoided by divesting himself 'as far as possible of a professional language – whether verbal or non-verbal – which cloaks our true being'.

In one chapter, typically titled 'Uncertainty', Lomas gives a long quotation from Turgenev's Rudin. This work struck him, I dare say, because it renders the insensitivity of a character who has 'an arrogant sense of certainty in his narcissistic preoccupation with his own performance'. In this fictional episode one experiences the kind of brash and open comment from which such a sensitive practitioner as Lomas perpetually shrinks. As he says, before introducing this long passage, 'it plays into the hands of those of us who seek to escape reality by denying the fact that humility is essential to the gradual and very complex journey to our understanding of each other' (Lomas, 1982: 122).

In later works Peter Lomas is more bold in placing himself in a new position, *vis-à-vis* the traditional stance of psychotherapy. 'I find that I am deeply and consistently moved by a desire to emphasize, in a way that psychoanalysis does not, the intrinsic worth of a personal relationship' (Lomas, 1994: 1).

Perhaps the most radical chapter of all is Chapter 13 of Cultivating Intuition, in which Lomas reflects on the nature of psychotherapy and his role in it. It is headed 'Ordinariness'. He reports on the difference in his conversation with a patient whom he telephoned to discuss a change in session time. This patient exclaimed how he sounded quite different: 'so friendly and relaxed. It's not that you're rude in sessions, but you are reserved and predictable. Now you're all over the place and it's great to talk to you'. Lomas explains: 'At work I find myself easily falling into a routinized and relatively restrained way of being . . .' (Lomas, 1994: 131). He reckons that 'some of our patients need us . . . to be godlike'. If a psychotherapist lapses, to reveal an idiosyncrasy or make a simple mistake, 'they are more likely to take comfort from the observation than be disturbed by it'.

> I conclude, therefore, that our assiduousness, and largely unconscious, attempt to appear special, have less rational roots: they are a function of a personal narcissism which is enhanced by the vanities of our profession. (Lomas, 1994: 131).

Lomas opts for a kind of relationship in therapy that is not detached: he quotes a colleague who declared 'I do not try to get to know my patients' and plainly disapproves. 'It may be useful', he declares, 'to conceive of psychotherapy as an attempt, on both sides, to make a relationship'. He believes that his contribution to this need is to 'demystify the practice of psychotherapy, and to recognise that the experiences within it are not only part of the natural world but can be encompassed by our ordinary capacities for experience' (Lomas, 1994: 134).

Lomas's approach to the conduct of psychotherapy may be said to be at the opposite pole from the manifestations he castigates in *The Limits of Interpretation* (1987b), where he has a chapter on 'The Mis-use of Therapeutic Power':

> Unhappily in our society there are many people and many groups who believe that they have a capacity, technique, message or knowledge that fortifies an arrogant intrusion upon the privacy of other people's inner lives. (Lomas, 1994: 111)

People tend to be easily seduced into such movements: 'Throughout history such groups have made an appearance in one form or another, and with various degrees of viciousness and cynicism' (Lomas, 1994: 111).

The work of Freud and his heirs, and of the Behaviourists, can be and has been used to dominate rather than heal, often by 'condemning people's respect for their conscious perceptions' This accounts for Peter Lomas's persistent honesty, and his struggle to discuss his work without pomposity or self-delusion. This impulse makes his writing a manifestation of what T S Eliot called 'terrifying honesty', as when he even admits that

> I believe, in general, it is wrong for therapist and patient to sleep together: but I would not exclude the possibility that such an event might be the best outcome of the encounter. (Lomas, 1987b: 138)

What is endearing in Peter Lomas, and makes his writing so genuine and profitable, is his refusal to set himself up as anything special: 'the moral content of the therapist's judgement is no different from, and no more authentic than, that of other people: what is different is the way it is exercised' (Lomas, 1987b: 148). This refusal to make his understanding and experience a basis for any kind of self-aggrandisement, while offering deep insights into human frailty, is something that today we should particularly honour.

Chapter 8
Peter Lomas and the question of science

PETER L. RUDNYTSKY

To anyone who has read the work of the man whom we honour with this volume – or, even better, had the pleasure of meeting him personally – it will be easy to sympathize with the dream of his patient, Ruth, in which she imagines coming for her session only to find that she will be seen by someone other than her usual therapist, and protests: 'But I don't want just a psychotherapist, I want Peter Lomas' (1981: 56). Or in the words of a reviewer quoted on the back cover of *The Psychotherapy of Everyday Life:* 'Reading this book will make you want to have, as well as be, a therapist like Lomas.'

There can be no doubt that much of Lomas's influence on the contemporary scene is due to his notoriety as an institutional maverick. Given the alpha status still enjoyed by psychoanalysts in the pecking order of mental health providers in Great Britain, and the widespread resentment harboured against them by less exalted beings – some of whom may have pursued alternative paths only after having been rejected for training by the London Institute – Lomas is to many people a singularly attractive figure by virtue of having first qualified not only as a medical doctor but also as a psychoanalyst, and then of having resigned from the British Psycho-analytical Society in order to practise independently as a psychotherapist. (Although he is the scion of a lower social class, the trajectory of Lomas's career parallels that of Charles Rycroft, his training analyst in the British Society, who likewise resigned out of frustration with the prevailing atmosphere of intellectual claustrophobia.) Having gained entrance to the most exclusive clubs, and then having chosen to dissociate himself from them, Lomas – precisely in virtue of his freedom from envy – makes an ideal spokesman for those (however justly or unjustly) embittered by the élitism of the psychoanalytic movement in Britain, while being a conspicuous thorn in the side of the Freudian establishment.

Peter Lomas, in short, is an extraordinary person in the world of psychoanalysis, above all because of his reiterated insistence that the practice of psychotherapy is not a matter of a specialized technique but rather an ordinary pursuit analogous to friendship. Paradoxically, it takes an exceptional person to be truly humble and willing to cast off the mantles of authority and expertise behind which too many clinicians of all ideological stripes are content to hide their emotional vulnerability.

Although Lomas has distanced himself from psychoanalysis and proposed that existentialism offers 'an intellectual framework that is more appropriate to the formulation of psychotherapeutic experience than any other' (Lomas, 1973: 87), the psychoanalytic tradition in which he was formed remains central to his work and constitutes the backdrop against which it can best be viewed. Beyond the immediate influence of Winnicott, whom Lomas justly calls 'the most creative thinker in the field of psychotherapy – whether inside or outside the psychoanalytical movement – since Freud' (Lomas, 1973: 69), and of the Independent group in British psychoanalysis generally, Lomas extends the heritage of Freud's most brilliant early disciples – Ferenczi, Rank, and Groddeck. In each of his books, Lomas pays tribute to the neglected work of Ian Suttie, *The Origins of Love and Hate* (1935).

The link to Ferenczi is the most obvious and important. In his introduction to the 1993 edition of *The Psychotherapy of Everyday Life*, Lomas singles out Ferenczi's 1932 *Clinical Diary*, which did not appear in English until 1988, as the book that has had the greatest impact on his own recent thinking. Lomas's introduction constitutes a landmark in Ferenczi's contemporary reception. He esteems Ferenczi because 'he placed the patient at the center of things' (Lomas, 1993: ix), and thereby posed a challenge to Freud's authoritarian conception of the analytic relationship. More than any other psychotherapist to my knowledge, Lomas has emulated Ferenczi's daring experiments in mutual analysis. He not only confesses his fallibility – 'When I think of the messes I have made – and continue to make – in my own life I wonder that I have the audacity to invite people into my consulting room and set myself up as someone who may help them' (Lomas, 1987b: 67) – but recounts examples of his clinical work. Of one patient, Margaret, who came to him after two previous analyses and whose first round of therapy with him had ended unhappily, but whom he agreed to see again after six months, Lomas writes: 'I told her about my childhood and the ways in which I had succeeded or failed to overcome my difficulties.' Margaret 'developed an increasing urge to help me with my own problems, and did whatever she could, directly or indirectly, to this end' (Lomas, 1981: 119–20). Similarly, he physically held another patient, Joyce, and answered her questions about his life unreservedly: 'Throughout this session, I again talked about myself and this time I quite lost myself in the telling of it, revealing some of my deepest anxieties' (Lomas, 1973: 145). In both cases, Lomas's self-disclosure had a beneficent effect on his extremely insecure patients and did not impair their confidence in his ability to function as a therapist.

Together with Lomas's resignation from the British Society, this championing of a radically egalitarian relationship between therapist and patient explains why he should occasion misgivings in more conventional psychoanalysts, but these same qualities of courage and compassion are what make Lomas the spiritual heir of Ferenczi. The extent of the affinity between them can be gleaned from Izette de Forest's tribute to Ferenczi, *The Leaven of Love*. As de Forest observes, 'Ferenczi allowed no artificial distance to intervene between himself and his patients, for he thought of them as friends . . . Psychoanalytic treatment, he thought, should take place as a natural, concerned, personal relationship, a part of life, not something removed from the experience of everyday living' (de Forest, 1954: 8). These are likewise the leitmotifs of Lomas's work. In the 1994 introduction to *True and False Experience,* he intimates how the therapist can hope to minister to a distressed patient: 'It is difficult to conceive of this response – which can only come from the heart – unless, with Ferenczi, we use the word love, however much it may embarrass us to do so' (Lomas, 1994: 5). That Lomas, like Ferenczi, proclaims the 'leaven of love' to be indispensable to the cure of souls is underscored by a biblical allusion: 'Just as man cannot live by bread alone, so he cannot live by taking thought alone: interpretation is not enough' (Lomas, 1987b: 5).

Lomas never examines his kinship with Rank or Groddeck, but it remains illuminating to consider. That these seminal figures have not been an influence on Lomas is symptomatic of their widespread neglect by contemporary analysts. On a single occasion, he refers in passing to Rank as having been, along with Ferenczi, the first psychoanalyst to question the efficacy of interpretation and to advocate the notion of the 'corrective emotional experience' (Lomas, 1987b: 72); but it is above all Rank's writings after 1927, when he had broken completely with psychoanalysis, that warrant comparison with Lomas's. In *Will Therapy*, Rank opposes Freud's 'ideological' therapy to his own 'dynamic' therapy, which 'in every single case, yes in every individual hour of the same case is different.' 'My technique,' he adds, 'consists essentially in having no technique' (Rank, 1929–31: 105). Lomas concurs: 'The uniqueness of every individual makes it impossible to formulate one aim or method of psychotherapy appropriate to all people in all situations' (Lomas, 1987b, 69). In his final period, Rank embraces a positive view of illusion, understood not in Winnicott's sense as a means of gaining access to truth but rather in Ibsen's sense as an alternative to it. 'With the truth, one cannot live,' he writes. 'At the moment we begin to search after truth we begin to destroy reality and our relation to it' (Rank, 1929a: 42). Again there is a meeting of the minds. In Lomas's words, 'Healing is not always commensurate with knowing the truth, for none of us can survive without illusions' (Lomas, 1987b: 145).

Unlike Ferenczi or Rank, Groddeck never belonged to Freud's secret Committee, but he was one of the most luminous first-generation psychoanalytic thinkers; and, with them, he laid the foundations for what became known as object relations theory (I hope to develop this thesis in a forthcoming book, *Reading Psychoanalysis: Freud, Rank, Ferenczi, Groddeck.*) Indeed, Groddeck's *Book of the It* (1923) is, in my judgement, a far more inspiring work than Freud's *The Ego and the Id* (1923) and perhaps the greatest masterpiece in the psychoanalytic literature. Even earlier than Ferenczi, who became his close friend, Groddeck underscored the need for humility on the part of the therapist. In this he is a precursor to Lomas. As Lomas admits, a disconcerting irony is inherent in the fact that the therapist 'is someone who sets himself up as one who helps others, who publicly announces he has the necessary qualities.' He adds: 'It is as if he were saying, "I thank thee, Lord, that I am not as other men: I am loving, kind and considerate"' (Lomas, 1981: 6).

These words allude, of course, to the parable of the Pharisee and the publican; the same scriptural text is a touchstone of Groddeck's teachings. Equating the publican with the It and the Pharisee with the I that blinds human beings to the conditions of their existence, Groddeck invokes the parable to expose the speciousness of all self-righteousness: 'Only now and then for a few moments is man, because of his human nature, permitted to beat his breast in honesty and to cry: "God be merciful to me a sinner"' (Groddeck, 1926: 173). Groddeck, however, does not content himself with exhorting his readers to emulate the lowly publican instead of the hypocritical Pharisee. Rather, he insists that he – like everyone else – is a captive of the illusion of the I and hence at once both Pharisee and publican. He concludes *The Book of the It* with the words: 'And only he is honest, who says, as that publican, "God be merciful to me." But do you not think that even this ultimate conclusion is pharisaical?' (Groddeck, 1923: 254).

Groddeck's sensibility may be more literary than Lomas's, but they share an appreciation of the precariousness of the therapist's position and both deflate the presumption of thinking one ever has all the answers. Groddeck never tires of reiterating that it is not the doctor who heals the patient, but rather the intrinsic powers of the patient's own unconscious that – if all goes well – are released by the therapeutic encounter. Lomas strikes a Groddeckian note when he advocates that illness be considered as 'an emanation of the patient's being, an expression of his aims and a meaningful aspect of his total life situation' (Lomas, 1973: 26). He writes: 'when healing occurs we can only take a limited amount of the credit: not only do the will of the patient and the facilitating situation of therapy play a significant part but there are always healing factors of which we know little or nothing, and (since life is enigmatic) can never hope to know.' Groddeck's term for these mysterious 'healing factors' was, of course, the 'It'; and, as the original 'wild analyst', he would doubtless have agreed with the continuation of Lomas's passage: 'Our task, in relation to Freud, is to be able to utilize those of his insights and recommendations which make sense to us today without feeling obliged to become converts to his systematization of healing' (Lomas, 1981: 20).

There is a further respect in which Lomas is Groddeck's lineal descendant. In the opening paragraph of Letter 1 of *The Book of the It*, Groddeck's persona, Patrik Troll, declines the request of his female correspondent that he eschew personal matters and be scientific: 'For what has my humble self to do with science? ... Perhaps, however, I shall meet your wishes if I tell you why I became a doctor, and how I was led to reject the claims of science' (Groddeck, 1923: 11). Readers of Peter Lomas might be forgiven for thinking that these words were his, for a central theme of his writings is his distrust – and repudiation – of science. In his introduction to *The Psychotherapy of Everyday Life*, he adduces his 'departure from Freud – and from science' as constituting 'much of the impetus for writing this book' (Lomas, 1981: 3); and in his 1994 introduction to *True and False Experience*, he retrospectively describes his first book as having been in part an attempt 'to find a way of thinking about psychotherapy that criticized the scientific, impersonal, and hierarchical approach' (Lomas, 1994: 2).

It is this last point that I propose to interrogate in the remainder of this chapter. As should be clear, I regard the work of Ferenczi, Rank, and Groddeck as indispensable to contemporary psychoanalysis, in large measure because it collectively provides an alternative to a narrowly Freudian perspective, which has hampered the development of psychoanalysis as both a theory and a method of therapy. I likewise esteem Peter Lomas as a thinker whose work has enriched the object relations tradition of psychoanalysis and a man of integrity to whom I would turn as a therapist were I in emotional distress. It is in this context that I would, in a spirit of friendly disagreement, raise the question of science in order to argue that Lomas's attitude is misguided.

My disagreement with Lomas is partial rather than total. As already indicated, I concur unreservedly with his conviction that the therapist should adopt an attitude of humility and openness – indeed reverence – toward the patient. His avowal that the practice of psychotherapy 'is less a science than a craft ... the aptitude for which derives more from a general experience of living than is usually supposed', and hence 'has much in common with teaching' (Lomas, 1981: 11) is likewise one that I would scarcely wish to contest.

Where then do we differ? The answer is in Lomas's assumption that there is an incompatibility between an adherence to scientific principles and the qualities of empathy and compassion that are vital to being a good therapist. I believe that Lomas goes astray in equating a departure from Freud with a departure from science – as though Freud's aspiration to be scientific should be numbered among his failings or, conversely, that the scientific method should be repudiated because of Freud's human limitations – and in conjoining the scientific in a triad with the impersonal and the hierarchical, as though these terms were interchangeable and equally opprobrious.

My own view is considerably more sanguine. While granting that the protocols of experimental science cannot teach one how to be a sensitive listener or tactful interpreter, let alone a wise and compassionate human being, I would still defend the proposition that the therapist gains immeasurably if he works from a theory that is grounded in sound science as well as in ordinary common sense. Bowlby quotes the aphorism of Kurt Lewin: 'There is nothing so practical as a good theory' (Bowlby, 1982: 37). Whereas Lomas's existentialism leads him to see psychotherapy as all art and no science, I discern no inherent contradiction between these facets of psychoanalysis. To draw an analogy from Christian apologetics, whereas Lomas wants to repudiate science as irreconcilable with the higher truths of revelation – as Luther did with classical culture – I would argue in syncretic fashion that science, like Dante's *Vergil*, is an invaluable guide for much of the journey, although it must eventually yield to Beatrice, or love, which alone can lead us to our ultimate goal of spiritual integration.

Although not decisive as to the merits of his position, Lomas's antipathy to science is at odds with the mainstream of psychoanalytic thought, and particularly with the independent tradition of object relations theory. Both Winnicott and Bowlby maintain that while Freud may have been mistaken in some important respects, he was right in trying to place psychoanalysis on a scientific footing. In a 1983 interview with Michael Neve, Clare Winnicott describes Winnicott's response to discovering the works of Darwin while a student at Cambridge: 'It changed his whole life . . . And he just felt, "There's a scientific way of working and that's where I am. That's what I want to do. I want to make discoveries and I want to understand them"' (Rudnytsky, 1991: 182). She reminds us of the great emphasis placed by Winnicott on the capacity to change one's mind: 'Once you're defending your position, you've lost sight of science, he would say' (Rudnytsky, 1991: 190).

For Bowlby, as for Winnicott, a veneration for Darwin as the prototype of scientific integrity underlies a more ambivalent relationship to Freud. As Mary Salter Ainsworth has pointed out, Bowlby 'was a great admirer of Freud's, in many ways. Freud's metapsychology really was an attempt to make a science of psychoanalysis, and Bowlby thought it was just too bad that he picked a Helmholtzian model rather than an evolutionary model' (Rudnytsky, 1997: 396). Two of Bowlby's late essays bear directly on the matter at hand: 'Psychoanalysis as Art and Science' and 'Psychoanalysis as a Natural Science'. In the former, he draws attention to the 'two very different aspects of our discipline – the art of psychoanalytic therapy and the science of psychoanalytic psychology' and seeks to give due weight to 'the distinctive value of each' as well as to 'the gulf that divides them' (Bowlby, 1979: 39). In his 1988 headnote to 'Psychoanalysis as a Natural Science,' Bowlby makes a wise observation:

> To accept that psychoanalysis should abandon its aim of becoming a natural science and instead should regard itself as a hermeneutic discipline has seemed to me to be not only a result of obsolete ideas about science but also a counsel of despair; because, in a hermeneutic discipline, there are no criteria by the application of which it is ever possible to resolve disagreement. (Bowlby, 1988: 58)

I would modify this by saying that it would be a mistake for psychoanalysis to regard itself exclusively as a hermeneutic discipline, as it is undeniable that psychoanalysts, like literary critics, spend many of their working hours interpreting linguistic utterances. None the less, Bowlby's larger point about the need for criteria by which to sort out valid from invalid claims, whether in the context of theory or therapy, seems to me fundamental. His essay concludes by acknowledging the inherent limitation that natural science 'deals in generalities but has little to say about singular specific events'. In the historical sciences, however, 'the individual example is the very essence of the case'. The latter can therefore never be predictive, or even fully explanatory. Thus, Bowlby elaborates, 'one is concerned to formulate general laws in terms of probabilities, the other to understand singular specific events in as much detail as possible'. As in the previous essay, Bowlby again proposes that psychoanalysis consists of 'two complementary disciplines' – one that tries to formulate 'general principles' of personality development and psychopathology, in which 'we adopt the criteria of the natural sciences', as we do when we try to define 'the essential features of effective therapy', and the other that seeks 'to understand the personal problems of a given individual and what events may have contributed to their development', in which we 'adopt the criteria of the historical sciences', although these are 'far from sufficient', if we are to help the patient (Bowlby, 1981: 75–6).

In light of the divergence between their views, it is perhaps understandable that Lomas should allude sparingly to Bowlby; but I none the less deplore that the only substantive mention of Bowlby in Lomas's books is a dismissal of his ethological approach to human behaviour as 'at least as mechanical as the theory that it seeks to replace' (Lomas, 1973: 68). In a 24 July 1987 review of Winnicott's selected letters, 'The Spontaneous Gesture', in the *Times Literary Supplement,* Lomas asserted categorically, 'psychoanalysis is not a science' (Lomas, 1987a:

798). This claim prompted a letter from John D. Sutherland, published on 14 August, in which he appealed to Bowlby's work as evidence that psychoanalytic 'theories about the early development of the person can be both verified and greatly enriched by studies using strictly scientific standards' (Lomas, 1987a: 875). According to Lomas, there is no reason to prefer Bowlby's belief in the primacy of the human need for attachment to Freud's libido theory, even though the former is supported by overwhelming empirical evidence (and conduces to both a more optimistic vision of human nature and a supportive mode of psychotherapy) whereas the latter relies on a wholly fictitious quintessence of psychic energy. Lomas justifies his rejection of Bowlby by noting that, in his system, 'free will is out'. This is, of course, an immensely complicated philosophical question. Suffice it to say here that, while Lomas may be right that most people believe that they have free will, and 'the degree to which they lack this belief is a measure of their illness', this does not mean that a belief in free will is therefore not an illusion. Certainly, an acceptance of the psychoanalytic axiom of the unconscious must render problematic – if it does not altogether subvert – an existentialist espousal of free will. Groddeck, though his antipathy to science is as extreme as Lomas, in this respect furnishes a polar alternative as he regards the belief in free will – like that in an autonomous I – as a form of hypocritical self-deception by which he, no less than any other manifestation of the It, is perforce captivated.

Just as psychoanalysis is at once an art and a science, so the most satisfactory resolution to the conundrum of free will may be to embrace a paradoxical double truth that grants its validity as a datum of subjective experience while doubting it insofar as human behaviour is regarded as a natural phenomenon. Be that as it may, I think that Lomas misses the mark in his critique of science as impersonal and hierarchical. These terms must be considered separately. As to impersonality, Lomas is right that the scientific method seeks to minimize the distortions imposed by what Bacon called the 'enchanted glass' of the mind in its attempt to know the world. But although the means of science are objective, the ends are not – or should not be – inhumane. To assume that they must be is to confuse a perversion of science with its proper use. The physician who strives to diagnose a patient's neurological disorder is not thereby rendered oblivious to his human suffering. Success in the former enterprise may rather be the precondition for meeting his spiritual needs. (For an exemplary blend of compassion for the afflicted human subject and fascination with the often-exotic efflorescence of neurological disorders, see Oliver Sacks's *The Man Who Mistook His Wife for a Hat* (1987).) As to hierarchy, the remarks of Winnicott and Bowlby attest that to be truly scientific is to adopt an attitude of humility in the face of experience and to be prepared to admit that one is wrong when the facts contradict one's hypotheses. Far from placing the therapist in a position of superiority to the patient, a scientific outlook should caution the therapist that the answers can never be known in advance and that the unfolding of the process of exploration ought to be awaited with a bare minimum of preconceptions. From this standpoint, Freud's fault is not that he was scientific but that he was not scientific enough, since – despite his sporadic protestations of suspended judgment – he is guilty of an obsession with fixed ideas to which he stubbornly adheres even when there is a paucity of evidence to support them.

Lomas's lack of interest in Bowlby is all the more unfortunate since their convictions are basically in accord in many respects. Lomas, for example, agrees with Bowlby that the extreme hermeneutic conception of psychoanalysis, advocated by Donald Spence, amounts to a 'counsel of despair' since it makes it impossible to establish 'a difference between truth and falsehood in ordinary experience' (Lomas, 1987b: 32). He finds reprehensible the fashionable tendency 'to regard the reconstructions in analysis as mere "narratives" bearing little if any relationship to past events' as a 'retrograde step – a by-product of recent literary theory – that lessens the chances of the child getting a hearing' (Lomas, 1993: xiv). What is ironic is that, although Lomas presents himself as an advocate of 'ordinary experience,' he relies upon a capacity to sift 'truth' from 'falsehood' which is, when codified as a set of formal procedures, the essence of the scientific method. Paradoxically, Lomas's antipathy to science undercuts the humanist principles he seeks to espouse and makes it impossible to counter the postmodernist relativism to which he is temperamentally opposed.

Two allied difficulties stem from Lomas's rejection of science. The first, as we have just seen, is that it logically precludes him from asserting that anything can be known with certainty. Thus, when he claims that 'a person aims, as Gestalt psychology has shown, to arrange in as harmonious and meaningful a way as possible whatever impinges upon him' (Lomas, 1973: 110); or that object relations theory 'corrects the view that the child's primary aim is the relief of instinctual tension and establishes the fact that he seeks a personal relationship' (Lomas, 1973: 112); or that the 'failure to put receptivity at the center of our work is incorrect in that it underrates the capacity of most people to grow if given sufficient time in relatively favorable conditions' (Lomas, 1981: 84) – none of these statements makes sense unless the words 'shown', 'corrects', 'fact', and 'incorrect' are given probative force. By turning his back on scientific standards of proof as a matter of principle, while continuing to appeal to them in practice, Lomas seriously weakens his own position.

The second, and subsidiary, problem is that Lomas misses out on numerous opportunities to demonstrate how cogent his ideas actually are. One of his most telling critiques of classical analysis is that the ideal of the analyst as one who presents a 'blank screen' to the patient is likely to do more harm than good. In personal relationships, he notes, such an indifferent response 'carries with it a negative emotional charge which must of necessity affect the attitude of the patient' (Lomas, 1973: 139). 'Contrary to the classical view,' Lomas elaborates, 'it would seem that an ordinary natural attitude to the patient provides a setting in which inappropriate responses, caused by childhood traumas, are more easily detectable' (Lomas, 1973: 140).

Lomas's searching challenge to traditional analytic technique gains corroboration from 'still-face' experiments conducted with babies between one-and-a-half and four months of age, which prove that they are capable of discriminating among facial expressions of emotion. When mothers fail to respond to attempts to engage their attention and present a blank stare, 'the infants usually begin to show signs of distress and protest, and they reduce their overall level of positive affect and often gaze in a different direction' (Vasta, Haith and Miller, 1992: 454). These findings have been replicated with clinically depressed mothers. These, likewise, do not synchronize in face-to-face interactions with their babies, who as a result spend more time crying or emitting other signals of distress (Vasta *et al.*, 1992: 455).

It follows from these studies that the patient is likely to experience the 'blank screen' of the classical analyst as a re-enactment of the 'still face' of the unattuned mother, and the anger or depression to which this type of analyst gives rise will reawaken the confusion of the bewildered infant. That Lomas does not appeal to developmental psychologists as his natural allies in pleading for 'an ordinary natural attitude' in therapy might seem to be no more than a sin of omission. But in his discussion of Bowlby, Lomas states that he has 'charted areas (which we share with animals) lying beyond the realm of decision – such as, for instance, the automatic smiling response of the infant to a human face or a mask resembling a face' (Lomas, 1973: 69). The note of disparagement in this assessment is clear. According to Lomas, Bowlby's theory 'does not encompass the most significant areas of experience.'

Here Lomas's neglect of empirical research turns to outright hostility, and his existentialist commitment to free will causes him to take needless offence at ethology, which, like the theory of evolution, reminds us that humans have much in common with other species, especially the higher primates. Indeed, after censuring as 'absurd' Freud's view that 'babies are not explanatory beings' but 'begin life in a state of "primary narcissism"', Lomas goes on to charge that 'science – in particular biological science – has led us badly astray in our understanding of the experiences and aims of the mother and child' (Lomas, 1987b: 74 and 76). Although I agree that Freud's concept of primary narcissism is untenable, it is again inconsistent for Lomas to say so while disparaging science. Indeed, to ascribe Freud's blunder to biology is scarcely less fallacious than the theory itself. For only an ethologically based tradition of psychoanalysis, beginning in Hungary with Imre

Hermann and transmitted to England through Balint and culminating in Bowlby, has refuted Freud's speculations and placed our understanding of the mother–child relationship on a firm empirical foundation. This tradition is being carried forward today most notably by Daniel Stern (1985). That the smiling response of the infant to a human face – or the distressed response of the same infant when that face is blank – lies 'beyond the realm of decision' does not mean that interaction with the primary caretaker is not one of 'the most significant areas of experience'. On the contrary, the genetically pre-programmed capacity for emotional attachment – as well as for anxiety at separation and grief at loss – which reflects our commonality with other species is also, when filtered through our more powerful lenses of language and self-consciousness, an integral part of what makes us human.

In its broadest scope, my disagreement with Lomas revives a long-standing debate whose antecedents include the quarrel between F R Leavis and C P Snow earlier in this century. (For an even-handed treatment of this controversy in its historical and intellectual context, see Trilling (1962).) In upholding the cause of science, however, I do not mean to deprecate literature or to suggest that the relation between them should be conceived in adversarial fashion as one of 'two cultures'. Rather, what I have sought to call into question is Lomas's suspicion of science as an arcane and even threatening endeavour. While conceding that the armamentarium of psychiatry may be called upon to treat 'mechanical illnesses', he regards it as an 'inappropriate approach to other forms of human anguish' (Lomas, 1973: 42). And because he regards 'ordinary human qualities' to be of paramount importance in the practice of psychotherapy, he urges that 'the pursuit of biochemical research into, and treatment of, the mechanical elements of psychiatric illness' should be 'confined to those who had elected to work in this highly specialized area of study' (Lomas, 1973: 53).

Ironically, by severing science from everyday life, the body from the soul, Lomas reinscribes a Cartesian dualism with all its baleful consequences. To be sure, psychiatrists have been known to dehumanize their patients, but I would hope that this is the exception rather than the rule; and if compassionate people surrender the clinical field to the technocrats, the problem will only grow worse. In a recent paper, Lomas writes:

> If the brain is the physical dimension of human experience, it is as complex, as delicate, as individual, as is a human being. It is as beyond our understanding as are human beings, whose nature has eluded the efforts of the greatest thinkers in philosophy and literature. How arrogant we will seem to future generations. (1997: 17)

This is eloquent, and to some extent true, but in my view ultimately misguided in its characterization of neurological research. For though the questions asked by philosophy and literature are in the realm of value and meaning, and hence inherently unanswerable, the puzzles of the brain – as of any other organ – are empirical ones to which solutions can in principle be found. Both areas of inquiry are integral to the human condition. Far from it being 'arrogant' of scientists to seek to unravel their riddles, I think it is rather Lomas who succumbs to complacency in implying that the quest is not worth pursuing.

As an alternative to Lomas's polarization of body and soul, I would cite Kay Redfield Jamison's *An Unquiet Mind*. A memoir of her own ongoing struggle with manic-depressive illness, which drove her to a suicide attempt, and which was only brought under control by a combination of pharmacology and psychotherapy, Jamison's book includes a moving tribute to her psychiatrist, who 'taught me, by example, for my own patients, the total beholdenness of brain to mind and mind to brain' (Jamison, 1995/96: 88). Elaborating on this 'mutual beholdenness', she writes:

> No pill can help me deal with the problem of not wanting to take pills; likewise, no amount of psychotherapy alone can prevent my manias and depressions. I need both. It is an odd thing, owing life to pills, one's own quirks and tenacities, and this unique, strange, and ultimately profound relationship called psychotherapy. (Jamison, 1995/96: 89)

Like Lomas, Jamison is both patient and physician, a soul-baring advocate of mutual analysis. She believes deeply in the healing power of psychotherapy, but knows from her own experience that sometimes it is not enough. But whereas Jamison's dialectical position can encompass the truth in Lomas's humanism, Lomas's dualism forecloses the truth in Jamison's science. We need both.

Peter Lomas is the last Romantic of psychoanalysis. His works articulate the perennial anxiety that 'we murder to dissect'. But I think we may honour Lomas's moral vision while continuing to owe allegiance to the scientific and critical spirit of the Enlightenment. If analysis is leavened by love, we need not be petrified by the fear that it will ever pluck out the heart of our mystery.

Chapter 9
Freud in perspective: the problem of seduction

PAUL ROAZEN

Freud's 1897 abandonment of the theory he had held in the mid-1890s, attributing central significance in the origin of neuroses and psychoses to the sexual seduction of children, was momentous enough that both his devoted friends and ardent foes consider that to be the time when psychoanalysis arose as a distinct entity. Thanks to the survival of Freud's correspondence with his intimate friend Wilhelm Fliess we have an unusual record of the workings of Freud's professional thought processes. It is true that whether one reads Freud's letters as a young man, or those composed during the most painful years of old age, he continues to sound very much like he was during the years that have come to be known as the Fliess period. Freud was emotionally freer in writing to Fliess than he was apt to be in his more guarded later years, but the overall continuities and consistencies stand out.

Freud's official biographer, Ernest Jones, thought that the fall of 1897, when Freud first wrote to Fliess about the collapse of Freud's confidence in his seduction hypothesis, 'was a turning point in his scientific career,' and most students of the field would agree with Jones's assessment. Jones, however, took a propagandistic view when he maintained that the crisis connected with the abandonment of the seduction theory

> tested his integrity, courage and psychological insight to the full. Now he had to prove whether his psychological method on which he had founded everything was trustworthy or not. It was at this moment that Freud rose to his full stature. (Jones, 1953: 292)

Freud had characteristically abruptly changed his mind in such a way that he was able to minimize self-criticism, although others, including his patients, were not to escape blame. Freud, feeling more right than ever, plunged almost immediately into his theory of the Oedipus complex, and it is not surprising that Fliess, usually stigmatized as a wilder thinker than Freud, decided initially to remain silent about Freud's version of the significance of the Oedipus story

We can get something of the range of opinion about this incident in which Freud gave up his central emphasis on childhood seduction if we remember, first, that Jones felt that '1897 was the acme of Freud's life' (Jones, 1953: 294). Ronald Clark, unlike Jones an outside biographer, called his chapter about this 'Splendid Isolation: Disaster'. (Clark, 1980: 140) And Jeffrey Masson subtitled a whole book 'Freud's Suppression of the Seduction theory', as Masson alleged Freud's cowardice in the face of contemporary medical criticism (Masson, 1984). There was weighty significance to Masson's notion that Freud had suppressed rather than abandoned his early concept, and the difference in words gives an idea of what a curious world psychoanalytic history can be. All objects of devotion, religions in both the best and worst senses, become embroiled in terminological disputes that are bound to seem incomprehensible to neutral observers.

No one can know the exact frequency of the dreadful occurrence of the sexual abuse of children, either in Freud's time or our own; yet to argue, as Freud did, in writing to Fliess in April of 1896 and in a 1896 paper, that Freud had discovered the equivalent of the source of the Nile, was 'off the wall'. It is not surprising that Freud's 1896 professional audience, before whom he presented a memorable paper on the origins of hysteria, should have given him, in his words, 'an icy reception', or that the famous psychiatrist-sexologist Krafft-Ebing should have reportedly observed of Freud's theory: 'It sounds like a scientific fairy-tale.' Freud wrote to Fliess about what had happened and said that such sceptics were 'asses' who could 'go to hell, euphemistically expressed'. (Masson, 1985: 184).

Yet Freud jumped headlong, after giving up his seduction theory, only a little more than a year after this, to a conviction about the Oedipus complex, which he held more tenaciously than his earlier view. It has taken almost a hundred years of psychoanalytic revisionists, who have sought to revise and alter Freud's own mature commitments, to succeed in amending his version of Oedipal emotions. It is the case that in his last years he accepted the concept of the pre-Oedipus phase of childhood thinking, but I doubt that any reasonable outsiders would be likely to share our own respect for the ins-and-outs of those who have bobbed and weaved to change Freud's ideas without being excommunicated from the fold of the faithful.

So my own tack will be to try to approach this whole matter in the spirit of intellectual history; detachment seems to be relatively out of fashion these days, yet it remains, I think, a necessary scholarly ideal. It is always easy to make past figures look ridiculous in their thinking, but my objective is not to damage the reputation of any psychoanalytic pioneer, much less Freud himself. He initiated a revolution in ideas about human nature that continues to influence how we think about motives and feelings; studying his work, alongside that of his followers and rivals, is incumbent on anyone who wants to make sense of some of the most deeply contested controversies of the twentieth century. But I readily acknowledge, just as in reflecting on other historical or theological disputes, that it can take restraint not to smirk at some of the curious belief systems that were once entertained.

Freud's central publication on the sexual seduction of children was his *The Aetiology of Hysteria* (1896b). Earlier that same year he had published an article *Further Remarks on the Neuro-psychoses of Defence* (1896a), the first section of which was devoted to the problem of hysteria; Freud's introductory remarks there should be enough to alert one to the dangers of his infallibilistic way of reasoning. Psychoanalysis was, he held, a 'laborious but completely reliable method' that he had used in making 'investigations' which also constituted 'a therapeutic procedure' (Freud, 1896a: 162). Even after Freud repudiated the theories he expressed about hysteria (and seduction supposedly played a central part in obsessions and psychoses as well) Freud clung to the firmest conviction about the reliability of his methods. He waited until 1906 to acknowledge publicly, in qualified terms, that he had changed his mind, nine years after confiding with Fliess about it in private. It never seems to have dawned on orthodox Freudians that Freud's initial reasoning had provided realistic grounds for the iciness of the reaction to his 1896 ideas. By waiting so long to express his new position, I believe that Freud had helped to dig his own professional grave in Vienna. His early campaign in 1884 on behalf of the supposedly safe medical uses of cocaine left him exceptionally exposed to further medical criticism.

It is, I think, greatly to Freud's credit that he was struggling to move beyond the therapeutic nihilism that can be associated with an exclusive concentration on hereditary factors. Many of the same problems about nature versus nurture continue to arise in contemporary clinical practice. Further, Freud was on a path-breaking course in trying to penetrate, as a psychologist, behind patients' symptoms to their causes. In 1896 Freud was still, and this would last up to 1914, relying on the authority of his Viennese mentor Josef Breuer, even though their collaboration had come to an end by 1894. Freud in fact came to loathe Breuer in private, yet cited him approvingly long after their falling-out. The whole relationship between Freud's personal thoughts as opposed to his public behaviour is a complicated subject in itself; Henry James memorably understood the naïve American confusion and moralistic awe, a set of emotions that I happen to share, in the face of the complexities of European manners.

Hysterical symptoms, Freud had maintained, cannot arise from reality alone, 'but . . . in every case the memory of earlier experiences awakened in association to it plays a part in causing the symptoms'. (Freud, 1896b:

197). For years afterwards Freud continued to be, from today's perspective, too insistent on looking for a traumatic scene that might prove curative, but his overall concern with memories marked him from the outset as pre-eminently a psychologist.

Freud pulled no punches about the centrality of sex in his 1896 paper on hysteria: 'in the end we infallibly come to the field of sexual experience' (Freud, 1896b: 199). He cited 18 cases to support his position. (Jones was such a blind proponent of Freud's that he did not seem to realize how he was endangering Freud's position by the claim that these were 'fully analyzed cases' (Jones, 1953: 290), whatever that might be taken to mean.)

Freud was unusually persuasive in part because he anticipated possible objections. And he raised the point that what might have happened is that he had forced 'such scenes upon his docile patients, alleging that they are memories, or else that the patients tell the physician things which they have deliberately invented or have imagined and that he accepts those things as true'. Freud took comfort from the fact that 'only the strongest compulsion of the treatment can induce them to embark on a reproduction' of the childhood scenes. Nor did he shy away from saying, on his own behalf, that the patients had 'no feeling of remembering' such childhood traumas. 'Why should patients,' he asked, 'assure me so emphatically of their unbelief, if what they want to discredit is something which – from whatever motive – they themselves have invented?' (Freud, 1896b: 294). Fliess knew Freud well enough, and understood the impact of the psychoanalytic treatment setting as conducted by Freud, to propose later that 'the reader of thoughts merely reads his own thoughts into other people', a proposition that Freud felt rendered all his 'efforts valueless' (Masson, 1985: 447), and one of the central grounds for breaking their friendship. Fliess could not jump through each new hoop as rapidly as Freud could hold them up, and it ought not to be surprising if Freud's reversal on the score of seduction tarnished the standing Freud's method could have for Fliess. Still, it is noteworthy that in Freud's 1896 paper, he had proposed to cure hysteria 'by transforming . . . unconscious memories of the infantile scenes into conscious ones'. Such a procedure, once detached from the quest for the finite memories of specific experiences, comes close to what modern psychotherapy would be interested in. Freud attributed to hysterics 'a general abnormal sensitivity to stimuli', a 'high degree of readiness to feel hurt on the slightest occasion', which he attributed in part to 'a physiological basis'. Freud concluded his paper by asking that his concrete conclusions be accorded less attention than the procedure he was introducing. That 'new method of research', exploring 'processes of thought which have remained unconscious', was recommended by Freud as a 'new pathway to knowledge' that psychiatry would benefit from (Freud, 1896b: 211, 216, 217, 216, 220).

In 1905 Freud began publicly if guardedly to retract his seduction theory, presumably in a way that allowed his methodology to survive intact. I am not suggesting that Freud was proceeding with dishonest intent; rather he was so committed to the neutral validity of his approach that I think he really believed that reversing himself on seduction need not cast doubt on the validity of his method for arriving at what he called his 'findings'. In the course of his *Three Essays on the Theory of Sexuality,* Freud brought up the sensitive issues of his 1896 proposal about the central role of seduction.

> I cannot admit that in my paper on 'The Aetiology of Hysteria' I exaggerated the frequency or importance of that influence, though I did not then know that persons who remain normal may have had the same experiences in their childhood, and though I consequently overrated the importance of seduction in comparison with the factors of sexual constitution and development.

After having claimed what he could not 'admit', it seems to me that Freud immediately went on to do just that. 'Obviously', he concluded, with the hindsight of his new conviction about the significance of infantile sexuality, 'seduction is not required in order to arouse a child's sexual life; that can also come about spontaneously from internal causes'. (Freud, 1905a: 190–1)

Then once again, in a 1905 paper that appeared in 1906, Freud was more explicit about his retraction. His theory, he claimed, had culminated in the thesis: 'if the *vita sexualis* is normal, there can be no neurosis'. (He was not only restating his 1896 argument, but now begging the question of what might be deemed 'normal'.) Although he did not concede that any of his assertions had been 'incorrect', he felt 'in a position, on the basis of deeper experience, to correct the insufficiencies, the displacements and the misunderstandings under which my theory then laboured'. His material had been 'scanty', and 'happened by chance to include a disproportionately large number of cases in which sexual seduction by an adult or by older children played the chief part in the history of the patient's childhood'. In this way Freud explained how he had 'overestimated the frequency of such events', 'though in other respects they were not open to doubt'. Freud had also been, in his earlier work, 'unable to distinguish with certainty between falsifications made by hysterics in their memories of childhood and traces of real events'. Fantasies of seduction could be a means of avoiding memories of infantile sexual activity such as masturbation. This alleged 'clarification' supposedly 'corrected' the 'most important' of Freud's 'early mistakes' (Freud, 1906: 274).

At this point it is well to consider Freud's private 1897 explanation to Fliess about the rejection of his early theory of aetiology. He mentioned first his 'continual disappointment' in his 'efforts to bring a single analysis to a real conclusion'. Further, the fact that 'the *father,* not excluding' his own, 'had to be accused of being perverse' (Freud's father died at the age of 80 in October 1896). Thirdly, 'the certain insight that there are no indications of reality in the unconscious, so that one cannot distinguish between truth and fiction that has been cathected with affect'. Finally, 'in the most deep-reaching psychosis the unconscious memory does not break through, so that the secret of childhood experiences is not disclosed even in the most confused delirium'. (Masson, 1985: 264–5). Not one of these four 1897 points was included in Freud's later publications, but by then Freud was able to smooth over and harmoniously rationalize a serious disjunction in his thinking.

In Freud's 1914 *On the History of the Psychoanalytic Movement* he wove the tale of the seduction theory into the story of the origins of the 'cause' which had recently been, in Freud's view, 'deserted' by Alfred Adler, Carl G Jung, and their respective followers. He alluded to the significance of infantile sexuality, and 'a mistaken idea' that 'had to be overcome which might have been almost fatal to the young science'. Freud maintained that he had been 'influenced by Charcot's view of the traumatic origin of hysteria', which led Freud to be 'readily inclined to accept as true and aetiologically significant the statements made by patients in which they ascribed their symptoms to passive sexual experiences in the first years of childhood – to put it bluntly, to seduction'. (Notice that Freud no longer mentions the objections patients had, overcome 'only by the strongest compulsion of the treatment'.) This etiology of seduction had broken 'down under the weight of its own improbability and contradiction in definitely ascertainable circumstances', a mysterious-enough explanation. Freud had been ingenious in the way he was able to correct his own mistake, although today it may seem as if he were too confident about how he resolved the problem. By taking 'psychical reality . . . into account alongside practical reality', Freud could give weight to the fantasy lives of patients. But he cited the 1896 meeting with Krafft-Ebing in the chair, as if Freud had made 'ordinary contributions to science', and as if it were the simple case that 'assertions on the part played by sexuality in the aetiology of the neuroses cannot count upon meeting with the same kind of treatment as other communications'. (Freud, 1914: 17–18, 21).

In a 1922 paper, published in 1923, Freud referred to 'the error of greatly overestimating the importance of *seduction* as a source of sexual manifestations in children and as a root for the formation of neurotic symptoms'. It appears that, by then, Freud was willing to make an admission that he had denied in *Three Essays on the Theory of Sexuality*. Freud was now proposing that this 'mis-apprehension' about seduction could be 'corrected when it became possible to appreciate the extraordinarily large part played in the mental life of neurotics by the activities of *phantasy*, which clearly carried more weight in neurosis than did external reality'. (Freud, 1923a: 244).

By 1924 Freud was even bolder about acknowledging what had happened in 1896. In a footnote added to his *'Further Remarks on the Neuro-psychoses of Defence'* he acknowledged: 'This section is dominated by an error which I have since repeatedly acknowledged and corrected.' He conceded that he had in the early days 'not yet' been able 'to distinguish between my patients' phantasies about their childhood years and their real recollections'. But this line of argument was at odds with the proposition, communicated to Fliess, that it was in principle impossible to distinguish between reality and fantasy in the unconscious. He was admitting that he had attributed to seduction 'a significance and universality that it does not possess'. Overcoming this 'error' meant that he could then see 'the spontaneous manifestations of the sexuality of children'. Nevertheless, Freud wanted to insist that 'seduction retains a certain aetiological importance', which meant that 'some' of his 1896 'psychological comments' were 'to the point'. And that same year of 1924 Freud also added a footnote to his 1896 *'The Aetiology of Hysteria'*; when he had written about patients having had no feeling of remembering the scenes, Freud commented: 'All this is true, but it must be remembered that at the time I wrote it I had not yet freed myself from my *overvaluation* of reality and my *low valuation* of phantasy'. (Freud, 1896: n. 268; Freud, 1896a: 204) Once again, one can wonder whether Freud had provided enough of an explanation to get himself out of his earlier mis-step.

By 1924 Freud had already contracted cancer of the jaw, and knew concretely that his lifespan was limited; and in his *Autobiographical Study* (1925) he sought to mythify further the past of psychoanalysis. In the course of describing how he had come upon 'the fact of infantile sexuality', he brought up 'the error' into which he had fallen 'for a while and which might well have had fatal consequences for the whole of my work'. He no longer blamed the impact of Charcot's teachings, but rather vaguely cited that he had been 'under the influence of the technical procedure' that he then employed:

> Under the influence of the technical procedure which I used at that time, the majority of my patients reproduced from their childhood scenes in which they were sexually seduced by some grown-up person. With female patients the part of seducer was almost always assigned to their father . . . My confidence was strengthened by a few cases in which relations of this kind with a father, uncle, or elder brother had continued up to an age at which memory was to be trusted. (Freud, 1925: 33–34)

Freud never explained exactly which aspect of his 'technical procedure' had been at fault, or how he had proceeded differently in later years. His accusation about the role of fathers for his female patients was novel, although in two 1924 footnotes revising *Studies on Hysteria* he indicated that he had earlier disguised the guilt of the fathers in two of his case reports; (Breuer and Freud, 1893–95: 134, 170).

Freud's *Autobiographical Study* expanded on the significance of his having had to reject the seduction theory:

> If the reader feels inclined to shake his head at my credulity, I cannot altogether blame him; though I may plead that this was at a time when I was intentionally keeping my critical faculty in abeyance so as to preserve an unprejudiced and receptive attitude towards the many novelties which were coming to my notice every day.

Jones later expanded on the constructive uses of Freud's credulity, but neither he nor Freud ever adequately explained, in contrast to Freud's detailed letter to Fliess, exactly why Freud had given up the seduction concept. (By the way, no one has ever successfully accounted for just why Freud had ever made dreams so important.) Freud preferred to skate over what happened during the crisis in his thinking in 1897:

> When, however, I was at last obliged to recognize that these scenes of seduction had never taken place, and that they were only phantasies which my patients had made up or which I myself had perhaps forced on them, I was for some time completely at a loss. (Freud, 1925: 34)

In fact it took a while for Freud to propose that it was fantasies of the patients that were at fault, and he never sufficiently explored how he might have 'forced' the idea on them. Nor can it be substantiated, thinking of his letters to Fliess, that he was 'for some time completely at a loss'. Supposedly Freud's confidence in his 'technique and in its results' was severely damaged.

> When I had pulled myself together, I was able to draw the right conclusions from my discovery; namely, that the neurotic symptoms were not related directly to actual events but to wishful phantasies, and that as far as the neurosis was concerned psychical reality was of more importance than material reality.

This alleged sequence of events succeeded in becoming established in orthodox Freudian historiography. But whatever Freud might seem to have conceded, he was still insisting that he had not been responsible for arousing such fantasies in his patients: 'I do not believe even now that I forced the seduction-phantasies on my patients, that I "suggested" them'. Freud claimed to have simply 'stumbled for the first time upon the *Oedipus-complex* . . .' And 'moreover, seduction during childhood retained a certain share, though a humbler one, in the aetiology of neuroses'. Freud was taking away with one hand what the other had just given. In his retraction of the seduction theory he was reasserting a measure of its validity: at any rate this is how I understand his claim: 'But the seducers turned out as a rule to have been older children'. (Freud, 1925: 34–45).

Freud's repeated attempts to prop up the legitimacy of his early belief in the seduction theory also led him once to implicate phylogenetics, although this proposal has attracted little support from within orthodox psychoanalysis. The possibility of seduction was classed by Freud during World War I as one of the *'primal phantasies'* which are part of our 'phylogenetic endowment'. Supposedly, 'the individual reaches beyond his own experience into primaeval experience at points where his own experience has been too rudimentary'. So that the seduction of children would have once been among the 'real occurrences in the primaeval times of the human family, and . . . children in their phantasies are simply filling in the gaps in individual truth with prehistoric truth'. (Freud, 1916–17: 371) (It is perhaps telling that James Strachey, with his excellent editorial notes but a down-to-earth sceptical temperament, neglected to include the appeal to phylogenetics in his many references to the history of Freud's involvement with the seduction theory.)

I have not tried to exhaust all the references in Freud's writings to the issue of seduction. It might go without saying that the possibility of incest always remained a central part of Freud's thinking. Although Freud's 1897 letter to Fliess does represent a turning point in Freud's thinking, he never completely gave up his interest in seduction as a source of psychopathology, and he continued to accord it an etiological role.

In the somewhat tortuous steps by which Freud arrived at the formulations he put forward in his autobiographical study, there are several conclusions that stand out. Freud had no way of knowing then that his letters to Fliess still survived, and would one day appear in print. So he did not have to worry about the possibility that someday historians would be able to compare and contrast his own later accounts with a contemporaneous one. He was free to engage in legend-weaving that was designed to enhance the story of his early struggles. No possibility existed of ignoring his 1896 papers, and so he made a virtue out of necessity, describing an early mis-step as a tribute to his open-mindedness and a way station to his supposedly discovering the truth about the importance of infantile sexuality.

I do not believe that Freud was consciously being deceptive. He fully believed in the truths he thought he had uncovered, and deceived himself about his own role in producing those so-called facts that made up what he thought of as his 'findings'. Like other men of action, Freud was taken in by his own propaganda, and was ideologically blinded from acknowledging his own part in his early mis-steps. For him to have adequately accented the power of suggestion implicit in his practice of psychoanalysis would have meant conceding too much about the built-in biases entailed by his therapeutic approach. (Before World War I Jung had declined to blame suggestion although he conceded that the sexual trauma had proved 'to a large extent unreal':

> You may perhaps be inclined to share the suspicion of the critics that the results of Freud's analytical researches were therefore based on suggestion. There might be some justification for such an assumption if these assertions had been publicized by some charlatan or other unqualified person. But anyone who has read Freud's works of that period with attention, and has tried to penetrate into the psychology of his patients as Freud has done, will know how unjust it would be to attribute to an intellect like Freud's the crude mistakes of a beginner. (Jung, 1961: 95).

In 1925, Jung gave lectures in which he stated that when he 'met Freud, he said that about some of these cases, at least, he had been fooled . . . There is then a certain untrustworthiness about all these earlier cases' (Jung, 1989: 16). As a matter of principle, Freud could acknowledge the possibilities of the abuse of power in psychoanalytic therapy, but it was tempting for him (and others following him) to think that, despite everything, he had come up with a neutral technique that anyone properly trained could employ. To have started to acknowledge his own full participation in the creation of psychoanalysis – and this perhaps helps to account for his curiously long-lasting public deference to Breuer – would have been to admit the full subjectivity of what he had accomplished. No one can be fully self-aware autobiographically, and it does not reduce Freud's stature that he too has to be considered subject to mankind's propensity for self-deception. Yet one final text of Freud's leaves me baffled. In his *New Introductory Lectures on Psychoanalysis* (1933) Freud mentioned 'an interesting episode in the history of analytic research' that 'caused' him 'many distressing hours'.

> In the period in which the main interest was directed to discovering infantile sexual traumas, almost all my women patients *told me that they had been seduced by their father*. I was driven to recognize in the end that these reports were untrue and so came to understand that hysterical symptoms are derived from phantasy and not real occurrences. It was only later that I was able to recognize in this phantasy of being seduced by the father the expression of the typical Oedipus complex in women. (Freud, 1933: 120)

Note how he begins so distantly – 'the period in which the main interest was directed to discovering infantile sexual traumas' – as if he personally were detached from what happened then. Nowhere else had Freud ever maintained that 'almost all' his female patients had 'told' him they were seduced, and not by their fathers. What became of the effects of 'the strongest compulsion of the treatment', and the absence of memories? Did patients reproduce such scenes, and Freud's reconstructions put them together, or did they tell him of seduction? The contradictions between Freud's 1933 account, and what he wrote in 1896, are bothersome, and a source of personal anguish to me. (Others have earlier noted troubling discrepancies in Freud's published accounts: Cioffi, 1973; Israels and Schatzman, 1993; Schimek, 1987; and Borch-Jacobsen,

1996). Freud in 1933 did not enlighten us about what drove him to see that 'these reports were untrue', which helps explain why his 1897 letter to Fliess has been cited so often. He was mentioning the alleged culprit being the father at a time in the 1930s when he was increasingly able to recognize the early developmental significance of the mother.

The earliest orthodox Freudian view of the Fliess period, as illustrated by Ernst Kris's introduction to his edition of those letters, was that the abandonment of the seduction theory had been set off by Freud's self-analysis (Kris, 1954: 216). On the other hand, I have long felt that Freud's self-examination was stimulated by how he had gone wrong about the seduction theory. He did not, however, succeed in getting as far in autobiographical knowledge as one might like. A close examination of the seduction theory, and how Freud dealt with his doing away with it, makes for a slippery-sounding story. One almost inevitably wonders how regularly Freud cooked his own books. If, for instance, one were to look at exactly what Freud meant by the concept of *'vita sexualis'*, I would expect to find some intricately involved reasoning. To what extent were Freud's early critics correct in suspecting that he was being exploitive in his emphasis on sex?

I think we must conclude with a quandary. If Freud's 1896 account was accurate, then his 1933 version was misleading. Freud can be expected to have forgotten what he wrote to Fliess, but would not one suppose him to anticipate that future readers would look over what he had written in 1896? Another possibility exists: perhaps in 1896 he had overdramatized the resistances of his patients, in order to highlight the underlying truth that he then wanted to propound. But if he was straight forwardly 'told' about the seductions, why wait so long to unveil what happened?

The quotations that can be assembled are troubling in their inconsistencies. If, as some might think, Freud was a liar, he certainly was not doing a good job at it. Jones, remember, thought that the abandonment of the seduction theory was among other things a test of Freud's 'integrity'. I prefer to think that Freud was suffering from a form of emotional blocking rather than that he was lying; in any event it behoves us to be on our toes about each of Freud's autobiographical memories.

Having re-read the relevant passages in Freud for the first time in years, I am reminded again of how persuasive and charming his prose is capable of being. His mastery of rhetoric makes it easy to slip over the differences between Freud's claims at varying periods in his work. After repeatedly fudging matters, we are confronted with the starkly different 1933 claim, which would, however, be consistent with Jung's 1925 version. Like others with political objectives, it was easy for Freud to think that the end – the promotion of his 'cause' – justified the means. One need only think of the last days of France's François Mitterand to realize how easy it can be not only to function in the face of public and private inconsistencies, but to manipulate them for the purpose of self-justification. And Franklin Roosevelt campaigned in 1940 on the pledge that American boys would not be sent into 'foreign wars'; when asked at the time how he could make such a commitment, given the possibility that America might be attacked, FDR reasoned that then it would not be a 'foreign' war (Sherwood, 1950: 235). Guile is a key aspect to worldly success. Probably each of us, with our convenient memories, shares in the kind of personal myth-making that is troubling in great leaders.

Hopefully others will re-examine what Jones said was 'the acme of Freud's life'. Ernst Kris, whose editorial notes to the Fliess letters seem to me often superior to those in Masson's later edition, shared Jones's ideological blinkers, for he argued that Freud's 1897 letter to Fliess about his mistake on the issue of seduction 'tallies with that given in his published works' (Kris, 1954: 29). Such wishful thinking can be attributed to the need for self-deception that Freud held was so central to the human condition.

Chapter 10
The limits of technique in family therapy

EIA ASEN

The work of Peter Lomas has influenced therapists of all persuasions – including family therapists. This is hardly surprising as his early work in particular contains much evidence of 'thinking families', whether it be in relation to childbirth, to sickness or to the role of the family in identity formation (Lomas, 1961a; Lomas, 1965b; Lomas, 1967c). It is in his later writings that Peter Lomas critically examines psychoanalytic technique and the 'expert' stance of the traditional psychoanalyst (Lomas, 1987b; Lomas, 1993). This contribution looks at how the field of systemic family therapy and its techniques have developed over the past five decades and it also examines the shifting position of the therapist within the field.

From the individual to systems

Once upon a time in Palo Alto a group of researchers and clinicians got together under the leadership of Gregory Bateson (Bateson *et al.*, 1956) to study the patterns of schizophrenic transaction in family. Steeped in the psychoanalytic/anthropological tradition, the group studied families like insects or tribes, describing and analysing, in minute detail, interaction and communication patterns in families containing a schizophrenic member. They 'found' that it was the family of the schizophrenic that had shaped his thought processes, mainly through contradictory or distorted messages (Bateson, 1978). One discovery in particular intrigued the group of researchers: if the patient got better someone else in the family seemed to get worse. Somehow families appeared to require a symptomatic person so that they could function better. The symptomatic person, later on referred to as the 'identified patient', seemed to get stuck in the role of the ill person. The group also observed that, in many such families, everyone resisted change – even if that meant blocking the clinical improvement of the 'sick' family member. This peculiar 'family homeostasis' (Jackson, 1957) led to the group viewing the family as a system with equilibrium-maintaining properties, such as overt or covert conflicts, secrets, alliances and blatant scapegoatism. The emphasis shifted from the 'sick' individual (whose 'sickness' was from then onwards put in inverted commas) to the family as patient and, not surprisingly, the parents slowly became the new villains of the piece. The 'schizophrenogenic mother' was invented, soon to be followed by 'toxic fathers' and eventually it was the whole family that was seen as 'causing' mental disorder.

Peter Lomas was influenced by this transatlantic work as well as by the work of Laing and Esterson (1971), which also focused on the families of patients diagnosed as suffering from schizophrenia. Like Bateson and his colleagues, Laing 'found' that confusing and mystified communication patterns inside the family led to the ill person's distorted perceptions. It is curious that Laing himself has never really succeeded in describing his therapeutic approach in any detail. It is therefore difficult to determine what actual 'techniques', if any, he employed to address family interaction. However, there is little doubt that family intervention was a major ingredient of his approach, aimed at freeing the sick person from that very role he or she seemed to be forced to play in the interest of the family as a whole. Many clinicians in Britain and other parts of Europe were directly and indirectly influenced by Laing's visionary work, though families – and parents in particular – were generally less impressed: they simply felt blamed for the illness of their offspring. Family therapy gained the reputation of fostering a blaming approach and it was not popular. How much easier – and less upsetting for all – to put the patient into one-to-one treatment with a psychoanalyst or biological psychiatrist.

Psychodynamic thinking constituted the dominant discourse in the field of psychotherapy in the 1950s and 1960s and many family therapy pioneers happened to have been trained as psychoanalysts or psychotherapists. However, in order to develop a new language resulting in new conceptual ways of thinking about therapeutic work, familiar psychoanalytic ideas and techniques had to be relinquished if not exorcized. Mutative, transference-based interpretations were 'out', forbidden under all circumstances, and any talk about 'feelings' was actively discouraged. Instead there was an intense fascination with observable behaviours, looking at *how* family members communicated and interacted with one another rather than looking for more and more *whys*. Consequently the word 'why' was banned from the vocabulary of budding systemic family therapists: after all, the symptomatic member was part of a larger system that had 'identified' him or her as being 'the problem', serving a function within the larger context – the family. The question: 'why has this person a serious problem?' was replaced by a new formula – 'what is the function of the symptom for the family?' Soon new methods were developed to elicit such 'functions' and practitioners became more and more competent – and excessive – in speculating and hypothesizing about the nature of family disorder. Adopting an individual developmental perspective to explain symptoms and predicaments was, for the time being, banned – often with veiled threats of being excluded from the new and still quite exclusive club of systemic therapists.

In those days family therapists had adopted the idea of the family as an open system, with the individual family members being the elements interacting with one another. If people were part of a larger system and behaved according to a set of explicit or implicit rules, then there seemed little point in discovering the reasons why individuals were feeling or doing what they felt or did. Looking back now it seems that this shutting-out of traditional psychodynamic ideas and practice was probably a necessary developmental phase that the family therapy movement had to go through in order to develop a new approach. After all, it seems that adolescents have to reject the wisdom of their parents so that they can develop their own ideas and language.

Perhaps the biggest departure from the intimate setting of psychotherapy, with its honouring of private space, preserved by the boundaries of confidentiality, was the introduction of the one-way screen. The very idea that psychotherapeutic work could be 'public', carried out by a clinician and observed by a team of colleagues, seemed outrageous and threatening – not least to the therapists themselves. Suddenly it was no longer possible to 'edit' – consciously or unconsciously – the material one presented to the supervisor but the supervisor was there – 'live' – observing the session and able to change the course of the therapeutic work then and there. Sessions were no longer private and intimate and families did indeed question this most peculiar set-up. Clinicians struggled and provided all sorts of explanations for the new technology, claiming that 'two pair of eyes and ears can see and hear more than one'. What was not stated overtly was that seeing whole families was unfamiliar to therapists and thus a challenge to life-long practices. 'Safety in numbers' seemed an important 'principle' to guard against therapists' sense of becoming overwhelmed. In the early days of family therapy there were preciously few proven techniques available to anchor therapists and prevent their feeling of becoming lost in an ocean of confusing emotions and interactions.

Whatever the complex personal issues regarding screens and teams, there was a major reason for this new technology: gaining another 'live' perspective of people's interactions and communications. This could only be helpful; viewing things from different vantage points means seeing things differently – and this makes it possible to think innovatively. New perspectives produce new theories and one of the major discoveries was how interactions were interlinked and could be framed in more than one way. Moreover, videotaping family sessions and studying them afterwards allowed therapists to replay – in slow motion if necessary – how an interaction evolved and to study sequences in minute detail. Just as it is possible to analyse closely how a particular goal is scored in a football match by rewinding the tape and replaying the build-up, similarly it is possible to do this in family sessions. Moreover, when such an analysis is carried out together with the family, by looking jointly at segments of a session, it opens up enormous possibilities for starting to consider how certain 'goals' can be scored – or saved – in the future. It enables families and therapists to look at what preceded a specific behaviour or communication, how this affected other people in the room and how their reaction in turn affected further communications. When such interactions are linked to problem behaviour an opportunity arises to think of new ways of doing things, hopefully stopping the family 'record' getting stuck in the same groove. Challenging, disrupting and blocking dysfunctional patterns enables new forms of communication and interaction to happen.

One-way screens, teams of four, breaks during family therapy sessions for team discussions, designing formal interventions that were then delivered in a sombre tone to often perplexed families – this kind of 'package' took off in a big way in the 1970s and 1980s. Family therapists congratulated one another for being able to adopt 'meta-positions' not only in relation to families but also in relation to other professionals and colleagues who were seen by them as ploughing away in their limited, unenlightened linear ways. Many family therapists (including the author) believed that being 'meta-' was being 'better' and, needless to say, this arrogance did not go down well with colleagues who had different belief systems and practices. With hindsight this was perhaps a necessary adolescent phase that the systemic field had to go through, with plenty of acting-out and often healthy challenging of taboos. But, did any maturation take place subsequently?

Family therapy techniques and how to survive them

There are a number of famous and influential family therapists who have developed their own brands of therapy, which are instantly recognizable by very specific techniques and therapeutic manoeuvres. However, like their psychoanalytic colleagues, the writings of these well-known systemic therapists are frequently more orthodox than their actual practice. Of course, psychoanalysts are rarely observed 'live' in their clinical work, so it is often only through personal contact with one of their patients that one discovers that some of the famous analysts behave much more like human beings than their orthodox writings suggest. Peter Lomas is one of the few psychodynamic psychotherapists who has had the courage to write about the apparent trivia of interactions and interventions in the consulting room – ranging from a cup of tea provided for the patient, to encouraging 'ordinariness'. One can only speculate as to the effects of installing one-way screens in some of the well-known psychoanalysts' private consulting rooms: it is not improbable that the interactions with their patients might become less humane and more 'classical technique' driven if they knew that they were observed. After all, they are famous for their method, their product, and this is what needs to be demonstrated over and over again to a public that likes what it recognizes.

The situation is not all that different in the field of family therapy. The big international systemic stars give workshops – often with 'live' families – performing their method in front of audiences that would like to see what they have read about. Subsequently technique dominates such sessions – and even the video illustrations that we family therapists use are there to illustrate specific techniques, brands, hallmarks of the particular approach. Rarely do we family therapists talk about middle sessions – they are much too boring – even though they are the 'meat' of therapy. Of course, in order to sell one's particular brand, for it to be marketable, it needs to have specific characteristics, be instantly recognizable, neatly packaged.

This fits with the needs of aspiring therapists. They usually want little more than a framework and specific techniques, however crude, to hang on to, particularly when at sea during a session – like the survivor of a shipwreck holding on to a plank of wood. There is a whole 'menu' of such techniques available in the field of systemic family therapy and all of these can be learned, step-by-step. Some models of family work have been simplified to a degree that is almost embarrassing. The 'solution-focused' work, for example, is a fairly recent phenomenon, emerging in the climate of Reagan and Thatcher, who represented political ideologies that do not wish to examine the causes of illness and dysfunction, but instead look at solutions. It is hardly surprising that this approach (De Shazer, 1988) has found many followers, partly because of its pragmatism and apparent 'quick fixes', partly because it is a method that is rapidly learned. The model is based on the observation that symptoms and problems have a tendency to fluctuate. A depressed person, for example, is sometimes more and sometimes less depressed. Focusing on the times when he or she is less depressed is to focus on the exceptions on which therapeutic strategies are built and it is these exceptions that form the basis of the solution. Therapy essentially consists of encouraging clients and families to amplify the 'solution' patterns of behaviours, which then relegates the problem patterns to the background.

As in other fields of psychotherapy, there are a surprising number of family therapists who believe that a few techniques suffice to bring about lasting changes in all their clients and they assume that the same intervention would fit all clients. Until not so long ago these therapists became excited by the last workshop they attended where some international super-star (usually male) had demonstrated his latest set of techniques. A few days later these would be tried out on some unsuspecting clients and their families, with varying results. This is not to deny that the 'buzz' of seeing some innovative ideas demonstrated by a great clinician can be inspiring.

One of the great innovators was S Minuchin (1974). He postulated that the therapist's task was to intervene in such a way as to challenge family interactions and communication patterns that are perceived by family members or the therapist as 'dysfunctional'. This includes questioning absent or rigid boundaries between people, 'unbalancing' the family equilibrium by temporarily joining with one member of the family against others, or by setting 'homework' tasks designed to restore or undo hierarchies. This structural approach is very active, with the therapist encouraging family members to 'enact' problems in the consulting room. For example, if continuous, repetitive arguments are part of the presenting problem, the therapist asks the couple or family to 'show me how you argue', encouraging all the participants to enter into role and to select a particular subject they habitually argue about. The therapist might initially act as a 'catalyst', helping to get things going, but soon family dynamics take over. This allows the therapist to study 'live' what happens and how communications become blocked, ignored or distorted. The therapist may deliberately increase the tension in the room, allowing the family members to go beyond their normal limits in the hope that this will induce a therapeutic crisis and result in the family discovering new resources and solutions. Experiencing such a 'therapeutic argument' can be a very powerful experience for family members and it can be followed by analysing subsequently how it started and escalated. This allows clients to identify ways on which the next argument at home can be stopped from getting out of hand. Many families report that what they had intensely experienced in the consulting room could be easily transferred to their natural home setting. Characteristically, families report that the next time a similar argument started at home, each participant remembered the session, with an invisible videotape running through people's minds. This has the effect of getting each person to pause and reflect rather than act, making plans and taking action on how to do things differently.

Family therapists, whatever their persuasion, use 'reframing' as one of their major techniques. Like a traditional psychoanalytic interpretation, the perceived problems are put into a different meaning frame, which provides new perspectives and therefore makes new behaviours possible. For example, depression is no longer seen as being linked with early childhood deprivation or chemical disorder in the brain but it is reframed as a useful tool that controls the relative distance between partners ('if you weren't depressed all the time, you might find it very difficult to keep your wife so close to you'). Of course, depression in a couple context could be reframed in all sorts of other ways and it is the act of creating new meaning that can help people to free themselves from familiar ways of seeing and doing things.

The technique of 'externalizing the symptom' (White, 1989) can be useful, particularly when working with families containing children and adolescents. For example, an encopretic child can be encouraged to think of the soiling as his enemy 'Sneaky Pooh' who needs to be defeated. The help of the family is enlisted to devise strategies to trick this imaginary monster. Soon all family members join forces to outwit the symptom, which becomes the enemy of the whole family. This playful approach can be used with phobias, anxieties and psychosomatic symptoms.

Circular questioning (Selvini Palazzoli *et al.*, 1980) is another technique used by most family therapists. The therapist conducts the family session mostly by asking questions, seeking information about people, their differences and the various relationships and their specific characteristics. Such questions might, for instance, be triadic in that they ask person A about his perception of aspects of the relationship between persons B and C. Talking about this in the presence of everyone inevitably produces feedback from everyone, feedback on which the therapist bases his next questions. By responding to feedback from the individual family members the therapist enacts the systemic notion of the circularity of interaction.

Selvini Palazzoli (1989), in her later work, became increasingly preoccupied with designing an 'invariate' prescription, a specific intervention she believed should be given to all families after a few sessions. This intervention, which prescribes mysterious parental disappearance acts, aims at disrupting 'chronic' family organization and thereby temporarily creating a stronger boundary between the parental generation and their adult children. Palazzoli observed that this intervention, effective though it seemed in many cases, appeared to be of little use in quite a few others. This finding led her group to rethink the wisdom of the same prescription being given to every family irrespective of its presenting problems.

In the mid-1980s family therapists started rethinking their work in a major way and there was a move away from technique and prescriptiveness to what was later termed a 'co-constructivist (constructionist) approach'. This entails the critique of objectivity, namely the traditional scientific view that the observer (or clinician) stands outside the process observed. Instead, family therapists started focusing on how observers actually construct what is being observed. Technique, which had tended to result in prescriptive therapy, gave way to 'conversations', with family and therapist 'co-evolving' and 'co-constructing' new ways of describing the family system in such a way that it no longer needs to be viewed or experienced as problematic (Jones, 1993). In Peter Lomas's terminology it could be said that family therapy has become more 'ordinary' – or, reframed in the terminology of politically correct health politicians, 'more consumer friendly'. The characteristics of the 'new' post-modern systemic therapists are those of clinicians who are democratic and realistic about the possibility of change, with no wish to impose their own ideas, being alert to openings and curious about their own position in the observed system, taking non-judgemental and multi-positional stances.

From dogma to integration

Family therapists, particularly when working in big cities, are encountering ever fewer 'intact' nuclear families, given that nowadays multiple forms of committed relationships co-exist in our cultures. This makes the term 'family therapy' increasingly seem a misnomer. It is not necessary to have a family in order to work with (systemic) family therapy ideas: any relationship lends itself to this, hence the emergence of the new terms 'systems therapists' or 'relationship therapists'. Moreover, the term 'therapy' itself has come under scrutiny: it can imply illness and dysfunction that require cures. Not surprisingly, there are plenty of families that regard it as outrageous that they should be thought of as being in need of therapy with the suggestion that there is something wrong with them or that they are the cause of one of their member's pathology. Many practitioners now tend to use more neutral words to describe their activities and no longer refer to 'sessions' but 'family meetings' or 'family consultation'. It is left to the family and its individual members to decide who should turn up for the first family meeting. 'The family' might be invited to attend the first session, but whoever turns up will be seen. It is common for the number of clients attending the actual therapy sessions to increase over time from one person to as many as six or ten, including members of the extended family or relevant others. It is possible to provide family therapy without the family – as long as it is made clear that the 'therapeutic system' is kept open, ready for anyone else to join family meetings if and when it seems right for them (Jenkins and Asen, 1992).

Family therapists, perhaps more than other psychotherapists, have in recent years become increasingly preoccupied with gender, race and class issues and how these affect clinical practice. Since the systemic therapies are concerned with viewing people and their presenting problems in multiple contexts, this is not a surprising development as gender assumptions, racism and class prejudice are all-powerful determinants of behaviour. Many family therapists have started examining their own professional attitudes in relation to these issues and more sensitive and appropriate practices are developing, both when consulting with individual clients or families and when dealing with the larger professional networks.

Now that family therapists have developed methods of good practice, family therapy is no longer confined to special rooms equipped with one-way mirrors, videos, microphones and teams of four. Systemic work is now done in such diverse settings as general practice, social services departments, mediation services, paediatrics, schools – and people's homes. Home-based family work is taking off in a big way, carrying out the work precisely in the contexts where problems manifest themselves. Here it becomes immediately evident how individuals and families live in social and emotional isolation. Family therapists try to connect families with one another and multi-family group work is gaining more impetus, particularly in the field of child abuse and neglect (Asen *et al.*, 1989) and with families containing chronically ill members.

The majority of family therapists have found their own therapeutic blend, drawing on a whole range of different ideas and practices. Many have rediscovered the individual and are attempting to integrate psychodynamic and systemic thinking. Gone are the days when psychodynamic ideas were banned from the vocabulary of self-respecting systemic therapists. Cecchin *et al.* (1992) remind us that a healthy irreverence towards one's own ideas is a necessity for any therapist to ensure flexibility and creativity. Once therapists fall in love with their models and believe these to be true and universal, complexity is likely to be reduced to some banal principles, with 'invariate' prescriptions or other entirely predictable interventions levelled at anyone, irrespective of their personal characteristics or family circumstances. Whilst such a stance may be reassuring to the therapist it is probably of rather limited value to clients and their families.

At the end of the twentieth century, psychodynamic and systemic therapies are no longer the strange bedfellows they once were. A mature relationship is developing between the two approaches focusing on how each can complement the other. Family therapy now operates on the interface between psyche and systems – or, as Peter Lomas's most recent book states in its title – on the interface of 'personal disorder and family life' (Lomas, 1998).

Chapter 11
A century of psychotherapy

DAVID SMAIL

Exactly a hundred years ago Freud was anxiously toiling to make himself a precarious living with a procedure for the treatment of neurosis which, in accordance no doubt with his hopes but scarcely with rational expectation, was to become, in the eyes of many, one of the defining features of the century to come. However, towards the end of that century, one of its most prominent historians could write an account of it which makes no reference at all either to Freud or to his creation, psychoanalysis (Hobsbaum, 1994).

Herein lies the extraordinary paradox of psychotherapy: on the one hand it is one of the great success stories of the twentieth century; on the other it is so insubstantial as to become almost invisible alongside the momentous and often terrible events and influences of our times. In one form or another this paradox constitutes a seam to be found running through just about every question that can be raised about the nature and status of psychotherapy.

So far as the Western world is concerned, the paradox arises centrally from our having lived with both an enthusiastic investment in the ideology of 'dynamic' psychology and a contemptuous dismissal of it on 'scientific' grounds. In other parts of the world, particularly of course the former Eastern bloc, there was no such paradox because, in the form we understand it, there was no psychotherapy. On a global scale, in fact, for most of this century the paradox was resolved into a simple opposition: one 'half' of the world (the capitalist) more than tolerated a belief in dynamic psychology which was, by contrast, anathema to the dialectical materialism of the communist 'half'.

Perhaps, indeed, this split throws some light on to the nature of our paradox. For the spectacular success of psychotherapy – never more so than at the present time – has been as a business enterprise. From early in its development, psychoanalysis (and later of course all the myriad variants it spawned) gained its warmest welcome in the pragmatic, commercial culture of the USA, and in the current phase of 'postmodernity' it is more than anything the *laissez-faire* philosophy of Business that has loosened psychotherapy from the strictures of a hard-nosed scientism that could find little merit in its procedures. It can, in fact, scarcely be disputed that psychotherapy is enormously popular (not just its practitioners, but probably the majority of its recipients would swear by it) and at the same time devoid of any convincing demonstration of its efficacy as a form of treatment for psychological distress.

Rather than seeing that we are confronted with a paradox made almost inescapable by the cultural and socio-economic influences bearing down upon us, we have tended to view the field of psychotherapy as merely problematic, and we have tended to try to solve the problem by one or another form of partisanship. Some, for example, have sought to settle the issue by ever more rigorous and sophisticated research procedures, others by embracing a confidently unscientific assertion of the transcendent value of the spiritual. We have split into rival 'schools' with, at times, positively fanatical conviction in their own version of therapeutic truth. However, no matter how damning the research evidence, or deep the theoretical splits, psychotherapy thrives. And the more impressive its growth as an industry, the more frantically we feel we have to show that it does or doesn't 'work'.

For anyone who truly wants to understand what is going on here, it is necessary to recognize that what we are confronted by is not just a problem that can, even if only in principle, be resolved, but a paradox which can be escaped only if we manage to 're-frame' it quite radically. I don't think this is nearly as challenging as it sounds, and will in fact demand of us no great intellectual sophistication. What is required, I believe, is a recognition that (a) so far in our preoccupation with psychotherapy we have been influenced more by interest (of the vested variety) than by intellectual honesty, and (b) that as far as 'scientific' understanding goes, most of the horses we have been flogging have long been dead. Further, it is precisely the interests that have been vested in psychotherapy that have fired the scientific zeal to 'prove' (or discredit) it, for in order to justify their making a living by their trade, therapists have for most of the past hundred years had to appeal to the judgement of the regnant intellectual power, and that power has of course been Science.

Right from the start therapists have been deeply ambivalent about the essential nature of their undertaking. In seeking to establish the ground for his enterprise Freud himself wavered between a late-nineteenth century mechanism, a barely suppressed belief in magic (see in this respect his letters to Wilhelm Fliess on the wonders of numerology (Masson, 1985)) and an authoritarian cult to be run by the inner circle of his beringed disciples. In fact, of course, psychoanalysis is now and always was above everything a business – an up-market brand that is careful to distinguish itself from cheaper and less exclusive forms of 'therapy' (a term regarded by many analysts as immediately indicative of an inferior product). Psychoanalysis, moreover, has as brand leader set the mould for pretty well all its competitors. Therapeutic schools are run more like businesses than sub-branches of science, and far from opening themselves up to a Popperian search for scientific validity, they seek to protect their hold on the market by all the forms of exclusivity known to the most insecure and self-seeking professions.

In their unremitting search for authority ('credibility', as our more cynical age calls it) the founders and leaders of the psychotherapeutic schools have proposed marriage to just about every available form of powerful intellectual ideology. If the phenomena of psychological distress had really turned out to be validly classifiable into the neat categories of medicine (and the temptation to adopt the medical model has never been wholly absent from the psychotherapeutic scene) they would no doubt by now have become the sole property of an exclusive and highly protected medical specialism. If the huge research efforts that have been made to wring from the data some indication of the unequivocal effectiveness of therapy had paid off to any consistently reliable extent, it is not difficult to imagine the nature of the ritual and rhetoric that would now surround therapeutic practice.

It is by now abundantly obvious that psychotherapeutic procedures are not amenable to any kind of conventional – or come to that unconventional – scientific appraisal, if only because it is impossible to define 'psychotherapy' in any reliable way or to determine with the remotest chance of consensus what its goals should be. Having become an industry in its own right, psychotherapy research will not go away, but no coolly rational mind can plausibly expect it to come up with any real enlightenment. However, even though the difficulties with it have long been recognized by thoughtful observers of the scene, there is no doubt that science has been the scourge of psychotherapy, and there is no doubt either that psychotherapists remain vulnerable to the kinds of attack launched by H J Eysenck in the 1950s and that find their echo much more recently (Epstein, 1995).

It may be true that at the present time, in the 'anything-goes' culture of so-called 'postmodernity', therapists and counsellors can begin to breathe a little more easily – but this is a precarious security indeed and, as Simon King-Spooner points out (King-Spooner, 1995), the field remains exquisitely vulnerable to the first ruthless policy-maker who shows up on the political scene determined to use science to undermine the position of psychotherapy. It is this kind of scenario that makes it impossible for psychotherapists to be honest about the ethical and epistemological dilemmas and contradictions of their undertaking.

Nowhere does this dishonesty become more apparent than in the hoops that therapists prepare for themselves and (more importantly) others to jump through on the question of becoming a registered profession. The unceasing efforts of psychotherapists to form themselves into some kind of guild which will protect their professional interests suggest that they are unlikely to follow the advice to live and let live (House and Totton, 1997) of that minority amongst them that eschews professionalization altogether. Sooner or later the more powerful groups among the wide diversity that is psychotherapy will come up with some formula or other that establishes their exclusive right to practise, and it will be built, precisely, on power, not on reason or reality.

As things for the most part are, and certainly have been, apologists for psychotherapy have had to adopt a number of rhetorical devices to underpin their cause. For example, the scientific validity of therapy has been hard to establish, it is maintained, not because there is none, but because the scientific procedures so far used in the investigation have been inadequate; once our techniques are sufficiently refined, the proof will no doubt be forthcoming. An alternative is to dispense altogether with the services of scientific method and to invoke instead other criteria of the validity of knowledge – the mysterious East, for example, may yield suitably impressive belief systems upon which we can ground our activities. For it does indeed seem that we are, with one or two notable exceptions, reluctant to practise therapy simply as a human undertaking to be evaluated in its own terms. We are uncomfortable without an Authority.

Another aspect of the paradox: the lessons of therapeutic practice teach possibly better than any other what it is to be human, and yet when we come to explicating and grounding the experience of therapy, simple humanity is not enough. More than anyone, it is probably Jeffrey Masson – that psychoanalytic renegade so reviled by his ex-colleagues – who puts his finger on why psychotherapy cannot be professionally practised as 'merely' a human undertaking.

In his book *Against Therapy* (Masson, 1989), having documented persuasively enough for anyone without a vested interest some of the abuses which inevitably attend the activities of those who conduct 'therapy' on the basis of a supposed superior insight into what is good for people, Masson goes on to suggest that if, as might reasonably be concluded, psychotherapy can at best consist in no more than a positive, beneficial human relating, then this is not something that can legitimately be professionalized.

It is at this point that even the most honest and best-intentioned psychotherapist gets stuck and is likely to find himself or herself falling in with the ranks of those who castigate Masson for his 'nihilism'. For the most honest and best-intentioned therapists are likely to be involved in professional practice and, precisely because of their good intentions and honesty, are likely to experience their practice as not only fulfilling for themselves but beneficial for their clients. In the light of their own experience, and however much they may agree with a lot of Masson's other strictures, they are likely to find that in seeking to deny them professional validity, Masson is simply wrong.

But Masson is not wrong. He has indicated precisely the crux of the paradox: it does not make any sense to try to professionalize what is after all only a kind of human relating. It would be as sensible to try to professionalize marriage.

Does this mean, then, that nobody should practise psychotherapy? I don't think so. What it does mean is that we have to reconsider the practice of psychotherapy and the role of the psychotherapist in the light of what has already been established about them from a century of intensive activity and investigation. We need to see, I think, that what we have come to consider the defining properties of professions – accreditation, training schemes, public registration, degree courses, and so forth – are not and could not be relevant to the practice of psychotherapy. The resolution to the paradox is to realize that psychotherapists can honourably practise their trade without being professionals. This, however, is no simple realization. It brings with it a host of implications of what would constitute the honourable practice of psychotherapy.

Psychotherapy is the distillation of certain aspects of human concern. It cannot be so much defined as indicated, discussed, exemplified. Nowhere is this done better or with greater honesty than by Peter Lomas (Lomas, 1981, 1987, 1994), whose favourite analogy for the therapeutic relationship is that of parents and children (though quite without the paternalism that this might be thought to imply). Many analogies can be made, and all with an element of truth – psychotherapist as parent, friend, doctor, priest, lover, prostitute – but none is quite right because no other setting and purpose is quite the same as that in and for which therapist and patient meet. And because it is like no other, one can but point to and describe what happens in this setting, what are its rewards and limitations, its freedoms and constraints. All attempts at reduction, regulation, definition and stipulation fail because they try to turn the therapeutic relationship into something it is not; above all, they try to render it impersonal.

Irreducibly central to the practice of psychotherapy is the psychotherapist himself or herself. This is just about the only consistent finding, consistently ignored, of the vast research literature on psychotherapy. It has been ignored, of course, because it does not fit in with the principal aim of the research effort, which is to establish a sound professional basis for therapeutic practice.

Even though the personal characteristics of your solicitor, surgeon, architect or accountant might not be a matter of complete indifference to you, you would probably not be wise to make them the first criterion of your choice of adviser. When it comes to psychotherapy, however, you would almost certainly be foolish to give overriding consideration to any other factor.

The psychotherapist reacts with the patient on the same plane of human relating, that is to say at the same moral and intellectual level. The one cannot, so to speak, encompass the other as, for example, the scientist can encompass the mentally inert data of his or her subject matter. (In introducing concepts such as 'the Unconscious' some of course have tried to establish a higher moral and intellectual plane from which they can look down on and encompass the patient as an object of study. A hundred years of reflection and research have, if nothing else, at least rendered this gambit unsustainable.) This immediately introduces into the undertaking an indeterminacy which is not only practically, but logically necessary – a personal indeterminacy of the kind written about so convincingly, though in another field of course, by the far-too-neglected philosopher of science, Michael Polanyi (Polanyi, 1958). In psychotherapy, however, the personal factor looms very much larger than in the natural sciences: it is absolutely central and overshadows the entire procedure.

The therapist himself or herself is personally the instrument of the process of psychotherapy.

Though, again, the analogy is not perfect, this makes psychotherapy more like an art than a science. The author of a work of art brings to it a variety of unique and unspecifiable components. No doubt techniques of painting and drawing can be taught, but 'being an artist' cannot be taught – even less 'being a Picasso'. The essence of being an artist is personal style. All that the leaders of the various therapeutic schools have done is describe, and then attempt – unsuccessfully – to codify and prescribe for others their own personal ways of dealing with life and relating to people. Freud, Jung, Rogers, Perls, Berne, Ellis have all tried to found professional dynasties based on what was in fact their personal style.

The absurdity of this lies precisely in the professional element. An artist might indeed become the focal point of a school of art of a certain kind, but no one in their right mind would attempt to patent the output, establish its scientific validity or set up a professional training course for its propagation. One need not quarrel with there being Freudians or Jungians or Rogerians as admirers and imitators; what is incredible is the notion that Freud, Jung, Rogers or anyone else embodied *the* way of therapeutic relating. This would be like asking which of Rembrandt and Goya was right.

There are lessons here that have been lost on all but a tiny minority of psychotherapists and among that minority Peter Lomas stands out like a beacon. For example, though perfectly prepared to instruct others in his art, he has scrupulously avoided any temptation to try to professionalize it and has unswervingly insisted on its essentially personal foundation. Consistent with that position, he has been far more prepared than most to allow those personal qualities, and their interactions with other persons in the process of psychotherapy, to be, through his writing, open to inspection. Most significantly, perhaps, he has achieved this without the kind of sentimentality and sanctimony that are the inherent dangers of any such undertaking.

As Polanyi establishes for even the procedures of scientific measurement, but to a far greater and much more visible extent, there are, in the conduct of psychotherapy, elements of the personal that cannot even be spoken. There is nothing mysterious in this, and nothing different from what happens in the indefinable play of subjectivity, the dance of the interweaving atoms of what Roger Poole called 'ethical space' (Poole, 1972), which take place in almost every human exchange. I say they cannot be spoken; perhaps what I mean is that they should not be, for to speak of them is like shooting birds out of the sky or hammering butterflies to a board. However much psychotherapy may be studied and written about, much of what actually passes between therapist and patient – and probably most of the most potent influences and insights – are mediated by personal elements which there would be no point in pinning down even if they could be pinned down, because they are unique to those involved. The deadening effect of what happens when you try to transform personal style into a blueprint for psychotherapy training was well demonstrated in the Rogerian school of client-centred therapy, where acolytes' attempts to emulate the master's 'reflection of feeling', etc., quickly became reduced to truly grotesque parodies in which 'mm-hmms' and repetitious summaries of what patients had just said became so empty of real personal feeling as to be almost unbearably embarrassing to listen to.

It is not, I should say, that one cannot study psychotherapy and even draw some generalizations from the observations made. What one cannot do is turn such generalizations into prescriptions for the detailed conduct of therapy itself. A century of psychotherapy has no doubt taught us a lot about the components of human relating which people find broadly 'therapeutic' – elsewhere I have summarized these as clarification, comfort and encouragement (Smail, 1993). But these are not factors specific to psychotherapy: they are merely part of the outcome of a procedure itself unspecifiable in some essential respects but shared with many other procedures. Part of what makes the 'good' psychotherapist special are the kinds of personal qualities which he or she might well share with the good doctor, priest, parent or friend; the rest is contributed by the unique factors of the social environment of psychotherapy (which do distinguish it from the clinic, church, home, etc.).

Many of the most important elements of personal relating in psychotherapy can be read only between the lines. This is not really a disaster, and the fact that content cannot be rigidly specified doesn't mean that important aspects of form cannot be identified. Though budding therapists may find it impossible to be, for example, a Peter Lomas, they may still be encouraged to be themselves. This is, however, not to say that simply 'being oneself' will inevitably have a therapeutic effect on others. How beneficial being oneself is will depend on the nature of the self that one is being, and while it is true that the therapist's 'self' is the instrument of therapy, the constituents of that self certainly cannot be ignored.

The central importance of the therapist as person not only demolishes the prospect of therapy as profession, but also presents a huge problem for the practice of psychotherapy altogether. For, if therapists cannot be manufactured, how are they made and how may we recognize them? In an age which has come to depend on, on the one hand (though decreasingly), official credentials and, on the other, advertising and public relations hype, choosing a psychotherapist on the grounds of what kind of person he or she is becomes an extraordinarily difficult, perhaps impossible, task. I cannot see any reliable way in which the process of choice could be formalized, and this because we have as a society destroyed the basis of trust upon which formal choices could be made – there are no institutions, sacred or secular, political or academic, where one can be assured of receiving the best available, informed and unbiased advice.

This leaves us with the informal channels of who we know, who's heard of someone, who we trust personally, or, God help us, who has the most credible website. There is no formal training in how to exercise personal judgement except, perhaps, in the most rarefied and protected corners of the academic world that have managed so far to escape the effects of market forces. People depend for their knowledge and their beliefs on the machinery of persuasion of the mass media, which are certainly not run in the interests of the individual. Most ironically, the various registers of psychotherapists that have been and will be produced are likely systematically to exclude the kinds of people most suited to the practice of psychotherapy.

Not that there is any one definable type of 'good' psychotherapist. Whom people find helpful in trying to get to grips with their confusion and distress will vary greatly according to their own experience of life. Up to a point it may indeed be the case that 'anything goes' and that there is a niche for all in the market place. I have known people be significantly helped by religious fundamentalists, fortune-tellers and rabidly authoritarian medics. But it is not just a question of helping some; there is also the possibility of harming others, and it is finding rules for minimizing harm that is both so necessary and so difficult.

There is no escape from the uncertainties involved in choosing a psychotherapist, but in this it is no worse than in many other fields of human choice. For example, what goes into the 'choice' of a favourite artist? One is not uninfluenced, certainly, by the culture of which one is a part, but there are also indefinable personal elements involved, which are felt rather than articulated. Indeed, there is an interaction in such situations between culture and person, public evaluation and private resonance, which is impossible to dissolve into its component parts. So with psychotherapy. It is likely that 'good' psychotherapists will have a public reputation, but it is also likely they will not be to everyone's taste.

One thing that does seem certain is that 'good' psychotherapists are very, very much thinner on the ground than would be indicated in the currently booming market in counselling and therapy. I suspect that this is recognized most clearly by those themselves forming part of the industry. Who would you go to if you felt in need of therapy? The answer to this question is likely again to highlight the personal element in psychotherapy. I can think of many eminent therapists I absolutely could not bear to confide in. Unlike the unfortunate user of the Yellow Pages, I already know who they are.

I can think of many qualities I would suggest for the good psychotherapist – experience, sensitivity, kindness, intelligence, knowledge, culture – none of which would be either necessary or sufficient as the basis of the therapeutic, but there is at least one that is both widely in evidence and absolutely fatal to effective therapy, and that is aggrandizement. Mystification, pomposity, and the authoritarian certainty of the guru, moral or aesthetic superiority: these are the qualities that seem to me to militate most seriously against both the beneficial practice of psychotherapy and the furthering of psychotherapeutic knowledge. But, of course, such evils are prominent features of every human undertaking and probably always will be. In the field of psychotherapy one may know them best by their absence – again, Peter Lomas's works are exemplary – but there is almost certainly no way of legislating against them. Human undertakings are vulnerable to all the human vices.

These, then, seem to me to be some of the lessons of a century of psychotherapy: psychotherapy is not and cannot be a profession; the practice of psychotherapy cannot plausibly or validly be accredited by training courses and university degrees; it is, above all things, a personal undertaking and cannot be reduced to a set of 'skills' to be transmitted on week-end counselling courses; the results of psychotherapy cannot be guaranteed.

This view of psychotherapy is of course one that is highly unlikely to survive in a world which is run according to the dictates of Business rationality, and the greatest danger is that the apparently inexorable urge to professionalize will stifle any further development of what I have called 'good' psychotherapy, if not kill it off altogether. The best hope for psychotherapy in these circumstances is that it can survive in the relatively informal practice of a small number of people with the nerve and the nous – as well as a number of the other rare characteristics mentioned above – to swim against the cultural tide.

Take heart! Was it ever any different? Nobody's ever been able to manufacture wisdom.

Chapter 12
The importance of being Peter Lomas: social change and the ethics of psychotherapy

DAVID INGLEBY

In this chapter I shall try to explain why I believe Peter Lomas's approach to be even more relevant now than it was over 30 years ago, when he started writing critically about the practice and profession of psychotherapy. I shall try to place his work against the historical changes that form its background – changes within both the field of mental health and the wider society. To begin with I shall attempt, albeit with some trepidation, to define what seem to me the key features of Peter Lomas's approach to the theory and practice of psychotherapy.

What is Peter Lomas's approach?

Fools, of course, rush in where angels fear to tread, and it would be a foolish person indeed who tried to sum up in a couple of sentences what Peter Lomas stands for. To begin with, over the years he has written many things about many topics: not only about the work of the therapist, but also about the profession of therapy and about issues in human development and human relationships. All in all, a substantial output – five important books dealing mainly with therapy, an edited volume (Lomas, 1967a, b, c) on the family, the recent collection of writings entitled *Personal Disorder and Family Life* (Lomas, 1998) and countless articles and talks. The surprising thing about all these writings, however – less surprising if one knows the man himself – is the high degree of consistency within them. By this I mean something different from playing the same tune again and again. There are many tunes, but in all of them we can discern the same fundamental themes.

There is another reason, however, for being diffident about trying to pin down the 'message' of Peter Lomas. If the message were that easy to define, it would be not be difficult to become a follower of his; and yet nothing is harder to imagine. If a person were to say, 'Hello, I'm a follower of Peter Lomas' we could be perfectly certain that they weren't;

somehow the line doesn't ring true, even though there would be nothing odd about someone introducing themselves as a follower of (for example) Sigmund Freud, Melanie Klein or Carl Rogers. Why should this be so? Because Lomas's attitude is essentially a Socratic one: like Kierkegaard, he condemns himself *by the nature of his message* to having no followers. Not answers, but questions; not dogmas, but doubts. Lomas's emphasis on the personal element in therapy implies, by definition, that nobody could ever tell another person how to practise it. This, however, has not prevented him from writing many well-read, much appreciated books about how therapy should *not* be done.

In the subtitle to this chapter I have referred to the ethics of psychotherapy because I believe this is the best way of defining what most of Lomas's work is about. His preoccupation is with the power of the therapist and the endless possibilities that exist for abusing it. His writings demonstrate a relentless scepticism about the very notion of 'professional expertise' in this area. Over and against this notion he places such concepts as common sense, ordinary humanity, intuition and humility – properties not listed in the entrance requirements of established schools of psychotherapy. For decades now, Peter Lomas has contrasted the notion of the therapist as a *special* person, possessing exceptional kinds of knowledge and skill, with a relentless emphasis on the *ordinary*: friendship, compassion, understanding, even (Heaven help us!) that four-letter word 'love'.

This commitment to 'ordinariness' is reinforced by his style of writing. However complicated the notions he is discussing – and he does not shy away from difficult psychological, sociological and philosophical issues – he scrupulously avoids jargon and always manages to render ideas in ordinary language. The fit between medium and message is perfect. If we had to define the common denominator linking his theoretical ideas, his style of writing, and his way of getting on with people, it might be this: an ingrained aversion to all forms of pretentiousness. In some ways, a very British attitude, but perhaps we can be more specific than this; is it not also a specially Mancunian one – the same down-to-earth scepticism about the antics of the high and mighty (especially those living in London) that for decades was the hallmark of the *Manchester Guardian?*

The most characteristic feature of Lomas's view of therapy is perhaps his chronic, incurable doubt about the possibility of pinning down the rules of good 'technique'. Technique might be acceptable, even compulsory, for a dentist or a surgeon: but the task of the therapist, defined at the most fundamental level, is to help other people rediscover their humanity – to make them feel human beings again. Such a discovery, in Lomas's view, can be facilitated only by offering them a *personal* relationship. As those studying infant development have realized, 'human babies become human beings because they are treated as if they already were human beings' (Newson, 1979: 208). This process does not rely on specially learned pedagogical techniques or biologically programmed repertoires of responses, but on 'the ordinary social responsiveness which human beings practise towards one another in intimate social intercourse' (Newson, 1979: 210). What is true for small people is no less true for big ones: but once rules of technique dominate the interaction, the relationship ceases to be a personal one and its humanizing potential is immediately reduced.

Such a message, of course, is extremely controversial, and that is what Lomas has remained all his life. To some he is a sort of latter-day Ned Ludd: like the leader of the gangs that smashed up agricultural machinery in early nineteenth-century England, he is regarded as a pathetically misguided idealist – and a rather dangerous one at that. For who would dare to challenge the benefits of professionalism and the regulation of technique? Does he *really* want a free-for-all in which quacks and soothsayers and purveyors of magic elixirs can exploit the helpless public? Does he really think that something as sacred as mental health can be entrusted to any Tom, Dick or Harry?

As I shall try to show in what follows, however, attitudes to professionalism have undergone a substantial change over the last half-century, and Lomas's work has both reflected these changes and contributed to them. In the 1960s, when his critical writings started to appear, public scepticism about professions in general (and the medical profession in particular) was beginning to increase: people began to realize that professions represent powerful vested interests. In the words of the medical sociologist Eliot Freidson (1976), they function as 'labour market shelters' that act to preserve lucrative areas of employment for their own members. This gives them a permanent interest in promoting an exaggerated image of their own competence and trustworthiness and in presenting their pursuit of their own interests as 'all in the interests of the client'. Whereas the 1960s ushered in an era of scepticism and put professions on the defensive, in the 1990s economic forces have come to their rescue. In an attempt to rationalize mental health care and promote cost-effectiveness, governments and health insurers have insisted on closer regulation of medical and therapeutic practice and have bolstered the power of the professions. Interestingly enough, however, this does not seem to have been accompanied by any increase in public confidence in the mental health professions. In a recent survey by the Dutch equivalent of the Consumers' Association, mental health care services enjoyed less confidence than any other form of health service provision: 73% of those questioned said they had 'little' or 'very little' confidence in the services provided (Consumentenbond, 1998).

The contrast with anti-psychiatry

Lomas's criticisms of the therapeutic establishment remind us inevitably of the themes of anti-psychiatry – and indeed, his work developed in the same period and the same intellectual climate as that movement. Though his own circle overlapped with that of the anti-psychiatrists, he never identified himself with them, and with hindsight it has become clearer why. Indeed, it may help us to define his 'message' to examine what the difference is between it and anti-psychiatry.

Although his critique shares many of the humanistic, person-centred assumptions of anti-psychiatry, one important difference concerns its object. Unlike anti-psychiatry, it is not directed at the reifying and dehumanizing effects of biological reductionism, but at the very practice that is supposed to offer an alternative to this: psychotherapy. It is this 'soft' sector that anti-psychiatry chose to ignore. Indeed, those whose only acquaintance with psychiatry is through the writings of Szasz or Laing could be forgiven for thinking that psychotherapy was hardly practised within the mental health services – that psychiatry's only answer to mental distress consisted of pills, straightjackets and electroshock. Recent analyses by historians of post-war mental health care (see Gijswijt-Hofstra and Porter, 1998) have shown how extreme this misrepresentation of mental health care was, and have offered some clues as to what motivated it.

It would appear that the anti-psychiatrists ignored the 'soft' sector because admitting its existence would have undermined their attack on psychiatry. This attack involved denying all the progressive tendencies within 'mainstream' mental health care at the time. A detailed study of historical sources by Jonathan Andrews (1998) convincingly demonstrates that instead of seeking to forge an alliance with his progressive colleagues, Laing hijacked their findings and denied their progressiveness, presenting psychiatry as though it was made up entirely of Kraepelinian die-hards.

Thanks to this tactic, a split developed rapidly between anti-psychiatry and the progressive forces within both in-patient and ambulant mental health care. For example, although there was considerable overlap between the humanistic ideals of the therapeutic community movement and those of anti-psychiatry, this movement was seen by Laing's followers not as an attempt to 'empower' mental patients, but as a grotesque reincarnation of early nineteenth-century 'moral treatment' (Ingleby, 1998). Laing's presentation of himself as the one good apple in a barrel full of rotten ones alienated not only the Kraepelinian old guard, but – more crucially – those who were attempting from within the profession to further more humane approaches and to understand mental suffering in its social context. In reality, anti-psychiatry was deeply rooted in psychiatry itself: Mathew Thompson (1998) relates it to the new thinking on mental hygiene brought about by World War II. Roy Porter (1998) shows that Laing was far from being the first to posit that families drive people mad.

Whatever role Laing's personality may have played in this misrepresentation of psychiatric history – and he does seem to have had, almost from birth, a talent for stealing the limelight – it also reflects, as Colin Jones (1998) puts it, the need of a movement seeking to establish its novelty 'to construct a heavily contrastive version of its opponent'. The image that Laing tried to purvey of a lonely, heroic struggle to liberate the schizophrenic from psychiatry would have been far less convincing if he had admitted that others within the profession were trying to do the same. From about the mid-1960s, indeed, anti-psychiatry makes more sense as an attempt to promote a 'counter-culture' in society at large than as a programme to reform mental health care. Laing may have started out with serious ambitions of changing psychiatry, but these ambitions soon came to stand in the way of the larger goal of changing the world. His role as evangelist for the new counter-culture undermined whatever ability he might have had to stimulate reform in the mental health system.

And because it was almost exclusively aimed at asylum psychiatry, anti-psychiatry's critique was out of date almost before it was formulated. Not completely, perhaps, because the bad old psychiatry was still flourishing: but it was rapidly losing ground to new approaches. By leaving psychotherapy as the unexamined alternative to asylum psychiatry, Laing fostered the illusion that misuse of power could not arise in it. Yet in the 1960s, the question of the power of the therapist was actually more of a burning issue than the power of the bullies in white coats, and this was an issue that interested Lomas much more than it did Laing.

The rise of the 'soft' sector

In the 1960s, mental health care was undergoing a radical change in its mode of operation. This change had begun at the turn of the century, most importantly through Freud's invention of the 'talking cure'. Psychotherapeutic approaches were developed on a small scale in the first half of the century, not only as a form of prevention – to meet the need for treatments that could be applied before a person had deteriorated so far as to need hospitalization – but also to provide a treatment that harmonized with the ethos of the middle class, which was rapidly increasing in size. It is worth remembering that one of the inspirations of the mental hygiene movement that, as it were, brought psychotherapy to power in the twentieth century, was the book *A Mind that Found Itself* by the Yale-educated Clifford Beers (1908), who experienced the inhumanity of asylum psychiatry at first hand. It was, above all, the middle class, with its burgeoning ethic of respect for the individual and freedom of self-expression, which balked at the oppressive and dehumanizing aspects of asylum psychiatry. The lower orders – who were used to being treated as objects rather than people – were assumed to be better able to cope with that sort of thing; what the middle-class citizen with psychological problems increasingly came to demand was a respectful, non-authoritarian, humane approach.

The steadily increasing growth of Western economies after World War II accelerated social transformations that had been taking place since the beginning of the century. In the period 1950–1975 these processes of social modernization were especially rapid. Changes in the moral and religious foundations of Western culture intensified the need for personal belief systems that could provide an answer to the question of 'how to live' The precepts of orthodox religion and traditional morality were rapidly losing their power to convince, and it was necessary to develop a new framework for understanding human relationships and the preconditions of human well-being. The new prophets of 'mental health' avidly filled this gap.

The transformation of post-war society brought with it a challenge to traditional authorities and institutions, in particular church and family. Traditional medicine also came under fire, for in more and more areas of social life, hierarchical social relationships were replaced by relationships based on negotiation. It was hardly a coincidence that the 'Amsterdam School' of sociology became the experts on this process, for these changes were nowhere so rapid and striking as in Holland. At the time when the work of both Laing and Lomas was appearing, a large-scale reshaping of mental health care was under way in all Western nations, in which ambulant care would come to eclipse asylum psychiatry as the major form of service provision. The ethos dominating the new services was middle-class and liberal – an ethos that also reflected the desire of mental health professionals to improve the image and status of their own profession. In the words of a Dutch sociologist, the medical sector today 'not only reflects middle-class values; it *is* middle-class' (Schnabel, 1998).

In a culture increasingly based on *negotiation*, the coercive, authoritarian methods of asylum psychiatry came to seem increasingly out of place. Indeed, in the whole field of health care there have been marked changes in the norms governing the interaction between professionals and clients. Doctors have become 'partners' and patients 'clients' or 'consumers', actively and intelligently concerned with their own well-being. Any form of violence, whether using physical or chemical means, is – at least in principle – out of place in modern health care. The mental health professional today is more likely to adopt the stance of a sympathetic friend and good listener than that of an omniscient expert. As a logical consequence of the reduced distance between professionals and their clients, ordinary people have come to identify themselves with the professionals, even to the point of reading their books (a process labelled 'proto-professionalization' by Brinkgreve *et al.*, 1979).

Viewed in this light, the rise of a person-centred approach to therapy was almost an historical inevitability. The chief figure associated with this shift is, of course, Carl Rogers. Rogers epitomizes the individualist answer to classical mental health care – the 'third force' that challenged behaviourism and psychoanalysis (asylum psychiatry being, for him, apparently hardly worth naming). The Rogerian ideals of 'unconditional positive regard' and a non-directive, listening attitude on the part of the therapist have spread to many more fields than that of 'client-centred counselling' alone. This enables us to pinpoint the approach of Peter Lomas even more precisely, for however much he shares Rogers' ideals, Lomas is not simply a Rogerian. The Freudian legacy is, for him, too valuable to be offered up on the altar of democracy. This would be 'a bridge too far', and in this respect his views are shared by very many therapists. What Lomas has above all set out to do is to reconcile the powerful theoretical insights of psychoanalysis with the ethical imperative of regard for the person.

In particular, Lomas belongs to the generation of 'post-antipsychiatric' writers who have concentrated their attention on the question of *power* in psychotherapy. Whereas anti-psychiatry had focused on the 'repressive' power of asylum psychiatry, the new generation of critics argued that Foucault's notion of 'productive' power was much more relevant to modern mental health systems: after all, most treatment is anxiously sought and gratefully accepted, and lay people respect and avidly consume the views of the 'psy-professionals'. In terms of democratic or humanistic ideals, psychotherapy may be a great advance on asylum psychiatry, but this does not make it politically neutral or ethically unquestionable. This applies especially to psychoanalysis, which as a technique is rooted in a society in which democratic ideals were a long way from being embodied in relationships between professionals and their clients.

Summing up, we might say that history has been on Lomas's side: given the changes occurring in wider society, it was only a question of time before 'the person' came to occupy a central place in the ideology of mental health care. Psychoanalysts, in particular, could not maintain a rigidly orthodox stance in relation to therapeutic technique while the whole of society (or at least, middle-class society) was changing so dramatically around them. Indeed, 'orthodox' analysts of the sort that Lomas so effectively criticizes are a dying race: an approach that might have been acceptable to patients in the first half of this century could hardly hope to remain so in the second half.

Irvin Yalom's best-selling novel *Lying on the Couch* (1996) describes, in a fictionalized way, the pressures on present-day American analysts to meet the demand for flexibility and 'authenticity'. The book's central character, Ernest Lash, takes his inspiration from the venerated and controversial Dr Seymour Trotter, whose technique is quite simple: to abandon all technique. Lash decides one day to try being 'totally honest' with his patients, and one might think for a moment that the ideas of

Peter Lomas had somehow found their way into West Coast psychoanalysis. Unfortunately, the attempt to be 'totally honest' leads to hilarious and sometimes disastrous outcomes – mainly, one cannot help thinking, because the characters who try doing it have been hiding behind their professional role for so long that they have simply forgotten how to be themselves. Whatever the reason, the result does not look remotely like the kind of interactions that occur in the pages of Peter Lomas's books.

If even the West Coast psychoanalytic establishment is flirting – albeit fictionally – with the abandonment of technique, must we conclude that the message of Peter Lomas is now redundant? Has the triumph of the historical forces favouring the personalization of professional relationships rendered his critique no longer necessary? Alas, the answer has to be 'no' because, as I shall describe in the following section, other opposing historical forces have also been at work. Somehow, all that emphasis on democratization and dialogue has not brought the ordinary person, and everyday empathic skills, into power – any more than is the case in public life generally. Other forces and factors have seen to that, and their existence is what makes Lomas today anything but a dated figure.

The bad news

In the first place, although anti-psychiatry may have driven the last nails into the coffin of asylum psychiatry, the ghost of Kraepelin has risen again: biological reductionism is as rampant as ever. The 1990s have seen the rise of a triumphant new version of biological psychology, based on spectacular advances in brain technology. (To some extent this triumph can be seen as a backlash against the exaggerated optimism over psychotherapeutic approaches in the 1960s.) The result has been a return to an alarmingly primitive medical model whose object is related not to the person but to his or her symptoms. Chemical manipulation of the supposed underlying processes is seen as the new panacea for all forms of human suffering.

The only difference between this and asylum psychiatry is in the style of the doctor–patient relationship. The new patient is likely to be on first-name terms with his or her doctor, and to have looked up the latest information about drugs and dosages on the Internet. In this Brave New World, people come to talk about their malfunctioning selves in much the same way that they describe the ailments of their car to the garage mechanic. Internet discussion groups are a fascinating source for the contemporary historian: on one such group, concerned with antidepressant use, I monitored the following chilling example of reification. A psychiatrist described how his wife's difficulties in waking up in the morning, caused by her heavy dosage of Prozac, had been solved by 'kick-starting' her with an injection of another drug! I had to wonder:

did he keep his Harley-Davidson in the bedroom and his wife in the garage?

Biological reductionism has undoubtedly been helped to power by the present financial crisis of Western mental health services. These services have become the victim of their own success: as the ideal of 'mental health' has become more widely taken over by lay people, the demand for treatment has come up against the ceiling of service provision, obliging governments and insurance agencies to implement tight management of the scarce resources. There is a growing demand for cost-effectiveness and 'evidence-based' remedies, which has had drastic repercussions for psychotherapy. Yalom (1996: 160) describes the results with grim irony:

> But deep therapy was losing the battle: the barbarian hordes of expediency were everywhere. Marching to the starched new banners of managed care, the battalions of brief therapy darkened the landscape and hammered at the gates of the analytic institutes, the last armed enclaves of wisdom, truth and reason in psychotherapy. The enemy was close enough for Marshal to see its many faces: biofeedback and muscular relaxation for anxiety disorders; implosion or desensitization for phobias; drugs for dysthymia and obsessive/compulsive disorders; cognitive group therapy for eating disorders; assertiveness training for the timid; diaphragmatic breathing groups for panicked patients; social skills training for the socially avoidant; one-session hypnotic interventions for smoking; and those goddamned twelve-step groups for everything else!
>
> The economic juggernaut of managed care had overwhelmed medical defenses in many parts of the country. Therapists in subjugated states were forced, if they wished to stay in practice, to genuflect to the conqueror, who paid them a fraction of their customary fee and assigned them patients to treat for five or maybe six sessions when, in actuality, fifty or sixty sessions were needed.

As a consequence of these economic forces, the demand for the 'rationalization' and regulation of therapy has become irresistible. Psychotherapy finds itself obliged to compete with biological psychiatry on the latter's own impoverished terms: the 'symptoms' to be treated have to be precisely delineated using a classification system (DSM) which is based on medical premises, and treatment has to be 'targeted' on these symptoms. In this model, there is no place for the insight that the definition of the problem is an ongoing process contributed to by both client and therapist. Rather, this is seen as proof of the laughably irrational nature of psychotherapeutic treatment. The only forms of therapy that can survive in this climate are highly formalized methods directed at specific symptoms, such as those listed in the passage quoted above. The only force that can oppose this tendency is the demand of consumers for a response to their suffering, which views them as they would like to be viewed – namely, as persons: by definition, this force can only be exerted by clients who are relatively rich and reasonably healthy.

This disquieting situation, which has been extensively discussed in a special issue of the journal *Society* to which Peter Lomas himself contributed (Lomas, 1997a) has put psychotherapists under pressure to change in ways that are quite the opposite of 'humanizing' or 'democratic'. What are strengthened are precisely the Mafia-like tendencies of the mental health professions: increasing pressure on members to toe the line, not to air their dirty linen in public and to stick to the protocols dictated by the management. If Peter Lomas were beginning his career as a therapist now, his sceptical, iconoclastic writings would surely earn him a penalty far worse than the polite disregard that has been his worst punishment so far. There can be no question, then, of historical forces having made his message redundant.

The power of the therapist

It is because Peter Lomas is acutely aware of the enormous power therapists can exert that he is so preoccupied with the need to exercise this power consciously and scrupulously. The nature of this power has also been the theme of the 'post-antipsychiatric' writers to whom I alluded earlier (see also Ingleby, 1985).

The critical study of the power of therapists perhaps began with studies by behaviourists anxious to prove that Rogerian 'client-centred' therapy was actually no more than a form of conditioning. Hans Eysenck, in particular, demonstrated with unconcealed glee that judicious timing of apparently non-directive reactions such as 'Hmmm' and 'I see' could influence the direction in which clients' utterances about themselves would change. Another critique was that of Kathy Davis (1984), who was concerned with the way women in therapy were subtly persuaded to redefine their problems as intrapsychic rather than external ones. Davis was writing from a feminist standpoint but, interestingly enough, the same process has been documented in recent research at Utrecht University on the interactions between refugees or asylum-seekers and their therapists. Here again, we see that clients who begin by locating their problems in the outside world (political persecution in their home country or oppressive treatment in the host country) gradually come to adopt the therapist's view that the 'real' problems are in their head.

This process of 'problem reconstruction' is perhaps at the heart of psychotherapy. Of course there are two sides to the question: factors both internal and external to the client contribute to most problems, and it is mainly the former, not the latter, with which therapists are trained to help their clients. While the process of problem reconstruction described above can degenerate into a form of 'blaming the victim', the process itself should not necessarily be seen as an abuse of power.

The point is, however, that there are forces at play that endow the therapist with more ability than the client to influence the outcome of the dialogue. Not only is the client in a dependent position, he or she may come to ascribe God-like wisdom and power to the therapist. An enormous amount of trust can be invested in the therapist – initially, at any rate, at the expense of the clients' trust in themselves. The question Peter Lomas never tires of asking is: does anyone deserve so much trust, and does the investment really have to be so large?

If we ask what motivates this investment, the answer will usually be in terms of the psychoanalytic concept of 'transference': powerful unconscious forces in the client induce a regression (the 'transference neurosis') in which the therapist comes to take the place of parent-figures *as they were experienced in childhood*. Indeed, Freud came more and more to the conclusion that the whole success of psychoanalysis depended on inducing and 'working through' this transference. In this way the emphasis on laying bare the transference and guiding its development has become the hallmark of psychoanalysis, in contrast to other forms of therapy that exploit the phenomenon but do not recognize its existence or its dangers. The counter-transference, too, comes under similar scrutiny. It is probably this uniquely self-critical attitude of psychoanalysis towards its own effects that accounts for Lomas's deep (and somewhat paradoxical) loyalty to it as a theoretical approach.

Time and time again, however, Lomas has insisted that there is a lot more to be said about transference. The role of God is so immensely rewarding that few can be trusted not to take advantage of it. Not all therapists, of course, are narcissistic power trippers – but those who have even the germs of such tendencies (and which of us does not?) can easily be seduced by the role. However, asks Lomas, is it not an offence against the patient as a person to allow them to treat one as God? Is it ethical to allow someone to fall in love with you in order to cure them of falling in love? Transference may be a necessary evil, but it remains an evil for all that.

I believe we should also examine the degree to which the role of the therapist as all-powerful, omniscient authority is *socially* constructed. To see it as something arising simply in the mind of the client may be another form of 'blaming the victim'. Individual therapists may be able to resist temptation, but can they do anything about the idealized notions that clients may have taken over from socially constructed images of therapy? Earlier I referred to the vested interest that all professions have in exaggerating their own virtues: in a competitive world, no profession can afford to advertise its limitations or to weaken its claim to truth. All professions, then, tend to cultivate an idealized image of themselves: and while analysts in training may learn to dismantle their fantasies about their own analyst, they are unlikely to come to terms with the fantasies that both parties may share about the profession itself.

In order to be able to explore these fantasies, trainers would probably have to distance themselves from their own profession much more than the profession itself would be happy to let them do.

I do not believe that the last word about this topic has been said by Peter Lomas or by anybody else, but we may be grateful for the fact that he has set down his thoughts on it so clearly and so extensively. As we approach the twenty-first century, it is clear that his critical attitude to those of us who have the temerity to tinker with the human soul will be needed more than ever.

Bibliography of books, chapters and articles by Peter Lomas

Lomas P (1959) The husband–wife relationship in cases of puerperal breakdown. Brit J Med Psychol 32, 117–123.
- (1960a) Defensive organization in puerperal breakdown. Brit J Med Psychol 33, 61–66.
- (1960b) Dread of envy as a factor in the aetiology of puerperal breakdown. Brit J Med Psychol 33, 105–111.
- (1961a) Family role and identity formation. Int J Psycho-anal 42, 371–80.
- (1961b) Observations on the psychotherapy of puerperal breakdowns. Brit J Med Psychol 34, 245–53.
- (1962a) The origin of the need to be special. Brit J Med Psychol 35, 339–46.
- (1962b) The concept of maternal love. Psychiatry 25, 256–62.
- (1965a) Passivity and failure of identity formation. Int J Psycho-anal 46, 438–54.
- (1965b) Family Interaction and the Sick Role, in JO Wisdom and H Wolff (eds). The Role of Psychosomatic Disorder in Adult Life. Oxford: Pergamon, 155–62.
- (1966) Ritualistic elements in the management of childbirth. Brit J Psychol 39, 207–13.
- (1967a) The study of family relationships in contemporary society: introduction, in P Lomas (ed.) The Predicament of the Family. London: The Hogarth Press and the Institute of Psycho-analysis, 9–25.
- (1967b) The significance of post-partum breakdown. In P Lomas (ed.) The Predicament of the Family. London: The Hogarth Press and the Institute of Psycho-analysis, 126–39.
- (1967c) (ed.) The Predicament of the Family. London: The Hogarth Press and the Institute of Psycho-analysis.
- (1968a) Psychoanalysis – Freudian or existential? In C Rycroft (ed.) Psychoanalysis Observed. London: Constable.
- (1968b) Taboo and illness. Brit J Med Psychol 43: 33–40.
- (1973/1994) True and False Experience. London: Allen Lane.

- (1975) The nature of psychotherapy. Tract 23. Gryphon Press.
- (1980) The gentle art of healing. New Universities Quarterly 419–28.
- (1981) The Case for a Personal Psychotherapy. Oxford: Oxford University Press. (2 edn, 1993, under a new title, The Psychotherapy of Everyday Life. New Brunswick and London: Transaction).
- (1985) What is a therapeutic response? In Current Issues in Clinical Psychology, Vol. 3. New York: Plenum Press.
- (1987a) Arrogant insights. Review of FR Rodman, (ed.) The Spontaneous Gesture: Selected Letters of DWW Winnicott. Times Literary Suppl, 24 July: 798.
- (1987b) The Limits of Interpretation. 1990, New York: Jason Aronson. London: Penguin Books.
- (1990) On setting up a psychotherapy training scheme. Free Associations: 139–49.
- (1993) The Psychotherapy of Everyday Life [new revised edition of The Case for Personal Psychotherapy] New Brunswick and London: Transaction.
- (1993) Cultivating Intuition. 1994, New York: Jason Aronson. London: Penguin Books.
- (1997a) The Durability of the Talking Cure. Society 35: 1, 17–9.
- (1997b) The moral maze of psychoanalysis. In T Dufresne (ed.) Freud Under Analysis: History, Theory, Practice. Essays in Honour of Paul Roazen. New Jersey: Jason Aronson, 125–30.
- (1998) Personal Disorder and Family Life. New Brunswick and London: Transaction.

Other Authors Cited

Abram J (1992) Individual Psychotherapy Trainings: a Guide. London: Free Association Books.
Abrams MH (1953) The Mirror and the Lamøp Romantic Theory and the Critical Tradition. Oxford: Oxford University Press.
Andrews J (1998) RD Laing in Scotland: Armchair Psychiatry and the 'Rumpus Room'. In Gijswijt-Hofstra M, Porter R (1998).
Anzieu D (1986) Freud's Self-Analysis. Trans. P Graham. London: Hogarth.
Asen K, George E, Piper R, Stevens A (1989) A systems approach to child abuse: management and treatment issues. Child Abuse and Neglect 13: 45–57.
Balint M (1979) The Basic Fault. London: Tavistock Publications.
Bateson G (1973) Steps Towards an Ecology of Mind. Harmondsworth: Penguin.
Bateson G (1978) The Birth of the Double Bind. In Berger M (ed.) Beyond the Double Bind. New York: Bruner/Mazel.
Bateson G, Jackson D, Haley J, Weakland J (1956) Toward a theory of schizophrenia. Behavioural Science 1: 251–64.
Beers CW (1908) A Mind that Found Itself. New York: Doubleday.
Bollas C (1989) Forces of Destiny. London: Free Association Books.
Borch-Jacobson M (1996) Neurotica: Freud and the Seduction Theory. October 76: 15–43.
Boss M (1963) Psychoanalysis and Daseinanalysis. New York: Basic Books.
Bouveresse J (1995) Wittgenstein Reads Freud. Trans. Cosman C. Princeton,NJ: Princeton University Press.
Bowlby J (1979) Psychoanalysis as Art and Science. In Bowlby (1988): 39–57.
Bowlby J (1981) The Origins of Attachment Theory. In Bowlby (1988): 20–38.
Bowlby J (1982) Psychoanalysis as a Natural Science. In Bowlby (1988): 58–76.
Bowlby J (1988) A Secure Base: Clinical Applications of Attachment Theory. London: Routledge.
Bramley W (1996) The Supervisory Couple in Broad Spectrum Psychotherapy. London: Free Association Books.
Breuer J, Freud S (1893–1895) Studies in Hysteria Standard Edition Vol II. London: Hogarth Press. (Penguin Freud Library vol 3.)
Brinkgreve C, Onland J, De Swaan A (1979) De Opkomst van het Therapeutisch Bedrijf. Sociologie van de psychotherapie, deel 1. Utrecht/Antwerpen: Aula/Het Spectrum.
Brook A (1994) Kant and the Mind. Cambridge: Cambridge University Press.
Byatt AS, Sodré I (1995) Imagining Characters. London: Vintage.
Cecchin G, Lane B, Ray WA (1992) Irreverence: A Strategy for Therapists' Survival. New York: Karnac Books.

Cioffi F (1973) Was Freud a Liar? BBC Talk.
Clark R (1980) Freud: The Man and the Cause. New York: Random House.
Coleridge ST (1811) Lectures on Shakespeare and Milton. In RA Foakes (ed.) The Collected Works of Samuel Taylor Coleridge Vol 5. Princeton,New Jersey: Princeton University Press.
Coleridge ST (1817/1974) Biographia Literaria. London: JM Dent.
Coltart N (1986) Slouching towards Bethlehem: on thinking the unthinkable in psychoanalysis. In Kohon G (ed.) The British School of Psychoanalysis: The Independent Tradition. New Haven: Yale University Press.
Coltart N (1996) The Baby and the Bath Water. London: Karnac.
Consumentenbond (1998) Vertrouwen in de Gezondheidszorg. Consumentengids 46: 28–31.
David K (1984) Problem (Re) formulation in Psychotherapy. Rotterdam: Instituut voor Sociale en Preventieve Psychiatrie.
Davis M, Wallbridge D (1983) Boundary and Space. Harmondsworth: Penguin.
De Shazer S (1985) Keys to Solutions in Brief Therapy. New York: WW Norton.
Douglas M (1970) Purity and Danger. Harmondsworth: Penguin.
Epstein WM (1995) The Illusion of Psychotherapy. New Brunswick and London: Transaction.
Ferenczi S (1955) Final Contributions to the Problems and Methods of Psychoanalysis. London: Hogarth Press.
Ferenczi S (1988) The Clinical Diaries of Sandor Ferenczi. Ed. J Dupont. Trans. M Balint, NZ Jackson. Cambridge, MA: Harvard University Press.
Forest De I (1954/1984) The Leaven of Love: A Development of the Psychoanalytic Theory and Technique of Sandor Ferenczi. New York: Da Capo Press.
Freidson E (1976) Profession of Medicine: Study of the Sociology of Applied Knowledge. New York: Harper & Row.
Freud S (1896a) Further Remarks on the Neuro-psychoses of Defence. Standard Edition. London: Hogarth Press, Vol. III, pp. 159–85.
Freud S (1896b) The Aetiology of Hysteria. Standard Edition. London: Hogarth Press, Vol III, pp. 189–221.
Freud S (1900) The Interpretation of Dreams. Standard Edition. London: Hogarth Press, Vols IV and V. (Penguin Freud Library vol 4.)
Freud S (1905a) Three Essays on the Theory of Sexuality. Standard Edition London: Hogarth Press, Vol III, pp. 123–245 . (Penguin Freud Library, vol 7, pp. 31–169.)
Freud S (1905b) Fragment of an Analysis of a Case of Hysteria. Standard Edition. London: Hogarth Press, Vol. VII. pp. 3–122. (Penguin Freud Library, vol 8, pp. 29–164.)
Freud S (1906) My Views on the Part Played by Sexuality in the Aetiology of the Neuroses. Standard Edition, Vol VII, 269–79. London: Hogarth Press. (Penguin Freud Library, vol 10, pp. 67–81.)
Freud S (1909) Five Lectures on Psychoanalysis. Standard Edition. London: Hogarth Press. Vol XI pp.3–57.
Freud S (1913) Papers on Technique: On Beginning the Treatment. Standard Edition. London: Hogarth Press, vol XII, 121–44.
Freud S (1914) On the History of the Psychoanalytic Movement. Standard Edition London: Hogarth Press. Vol XIV, 1–66. (Penguin Freud Library. vol 15, pp. 57–128.)
Freud, S (1916–17) Introductory Lectures on Psychoanalysis Standard Edition. London: Hogarth Press. Vol XV–XVI (Penguin Freud Library, vol 1)
Freud S, (1923) Two Encyclopedia articles. Standard Edition. London: Hogarth Press Vol XVIII pp. 235–59.

Freud S (1923b) The Ego and the Id. Standard edition. London: Hogarth Press, Vol XIX, pp. 1–66. (Penguin Freud Library, vol. 11, 339–407.)

Freud S (1925) An Autobiographical Study. Standard Edition. London: Hogarth Press, Vol. XX, pp. 1–74. (Penguin Freud Library, vol 15, pp. 183–259.)

Freud S (1926) The Question of Lay Analysis. Standard Edition. London: Hogarth Press, Vol XX, pp. 177–250. (Penguin Freud Library, vol 15, pp. 272–363.)

Freud S (1933) New Introductory Lectures on Psychoanalysis. Standard Edition. London: Hogarth Press, Vol. XXII. (Penguin Freud Library, vol. 2.)

Geertz C (1993) Common sense as a cultural system. In Local Knowledge. London: Fontana.

Genette G (1997) Palimpsests. Trans. Norman C, Doubinsky C. Lincoln: University of Nebraska Press.

Gijswijt-Hofstra M, Porter R (eds) (1998) Cultures of Psychiatry and Mental Health Care in Postwar Britain and the Netherlands. Amsterdam: Rodopi.

Groddeck G (1923/1961) The Book of the It. Trans. Collins VME. New York: Mentor.

Groddeck G (1926/1989) The It and the Gospels. In Collins VME. Trans. The Unknown Self. London: Vision Press, pp. 165–90.

Halmos P (1965) The Faith of the Counsellors. London: Constable.

Hobsbaum E (1994) The Age of Extremes. The Short Twentieth Century 1914–1991. Harmondsworth: Michael Joseph, Penguin.

Holmes J (1993) John Bowlby and Attachment Theory. London: Routledge.

Holmes R (1989) Coleridge, Early Visions. London: Hodder & Stoughton.

House R, Totton N (eds) (1997) Implausible Professions. Ross-on Wye: PCCS Books.

Ingleby D (1985) Professionals as socialisers: the 'psy complex'. In Scull A, Spitzer S (eds) Research in Law, Deviance and Social Control. New York: Jai Press, Vol. 7, pp. 79–109.

Ingleby D (1998) A view from the North Sea. In Gijswijt-Hofstra M, Porter R (1998).

Israels H and Schatzman M (1993). The Seduction Theory. History of Psychiatry Vol 4 23–59.

Jackson D (1957) The question of family homeostasis. Psychiatric Quarterly Suppl, 31: 79–90.

Jamison KR (1995/1996) An Unquiet Mind: A Memoir of Moods and Madness. New York: Vintage Books.

Jenkins H, Asen K (1992) Family therapy without the family: a framework for systemic practice. Journal of Family Therapy 14(1) 1–14.

Jones C (1998) Raising the Anti: Jan Foudraine, Ronald Laing and Anti-psychiatry. In Gijswijt-Hofstra M, Porter R (1998).

Jones E (1953) The Life and Work of Sigmund Freud. New York: Basic Books, Vol 1.

Jones E (1993) Family Systems Therapy. Chichester/New York: John Wiley & Sons.

Jung CG (1913/1961) The Theory of Psychoanalysis in Hull R.F.C. (tran) The Collected Works of C.G. Jung Vol 4 pp. 85–226. Princeton NJ: Princeton University Press.

Jung C.G. (1989) Analytical Psychology: Notes of the Seminar given in 1925 ed McGuire, W. Princeton NJ: Princeton University Press.

Kant I (1929) Critique of Pure Reason. Trans. Smith NK. London: Macmillan.

Kant I (1952) The Critique of Judgement. Trans. Meredith JC. Oxford: The Clarendon Press.

King-Spooner S (1995) Psychotherapy and the White Dodo. Changes 13: pp. 45–51.

Kris E (1954) Introduction to the Origins of Psychoanalysis, ed Bonaparte M, Freud A and Kris E. London: Imago

Lacan J (1966) Ecrits. Paris: Seuil.

Laing RD, Esterson A (1971) Sanity, Madness and the Family. New York: Basic Books.
Main M (1991) Metacognitive knowldege, metacognitive monitoring and singular (coherent) vs. multiple (incoherent) model of attachment: findings and directions for future research. In Attachment Across the Life Cycle. Edited by Parkes CM, Stevenson-Hinde J, Marris P. London: Routledge.
Makkreel R (1990) Imagination and Interpretation in Kant. Chicago: University of Chicago Press.
Margalit, A. (1996)The Decent Society. Trans N. Goldblum. Cambridge, Mass: Harvard University Press.
Masson JM (1984) The Assult on Truth: Freud's suppression of seduction theory. New York: Farras, Shaw and Giroux.
Masson JM (1985) The Complete Letters of Sigmund Freud to Wilhelm Fliess 1887-1904. Cambridge MA: Harvard University Press.
Masson JM (1989) Aganst Therapy. London: Collins.
Milner M (1969) The Hands of the Living God. London: Hogarth Press.
Minuchin S (1974) Families and Family Therapy. London: Tavistock.
Newson J (1979) The growth of shared understandings between infant and caretaker. In Bullowa M (ed.) Before Speech: The Beginning of Interpersonal Communication. London: Cambridge University Press.
Nietzsche F (1970) Aurore, Posthumous Fragments. Paris: Gallimard.
Polanyi M (1958) Personal Knowledge. London: Routledge & Kegan Paul.
Poole R (1972) Towards Deep Subjectivity. Harmondsworth: Allen Lane, Penguin.
Porter R (1998) Anti-psychiatry and the family: taking the long view. In Gijswijt-Hofstra M, Porter R (1998).
Rank O (1929/1978) Truth and Reality. Trans. Taft, J. New York: Norton.
Rank O (1929-31/1978) Will Therapy. Trans. Taft, J. New York: Norton.
Rayner E (1991) The Independent Mind in British Psychoanalysis. London: Free Association Books.
Roth S (1994) Review of 'Cultivating Intuition'. Journal of the American Psychoanalytic Association 42: 1299-300.
Roudinesco E (1997) Jacques Lacan. Trans. Bray J. Cambridge: Polity Press.
Roustang F (1982) Dire Mastery. Discipleship from Freud to Lacan. Trans. Lukacher N. Baltimore: Johns Hopkins University Press.
Rudnytsky PL (1991) The Psychoanalytic Vocation: Rank, Winnicott, and the Legacy of Freud. New Haven: Yale University Press.
Rudnytsky PL (1997) The personal origins of attachment theory: An Interview with Mary Salter Ainsworth. Psychoanalytic Study of the Child 52, 386-405
Rycroft R (1968) Imagination and Reality. London: Hogarth Press.
Rycroft C (1985) Psychoanalysis and Beyond. London: Chatto & Windus.
Sacks O (1987) The Man Who Mistook His Wife for a Hat. New York: Harper & Row.
Schafer R (1983) The Analytic Attitude. London: Hogarth Press.
Schnabel P (1998) Dutch psychiatry after World War Two: an overview. In Gifswijt-Horstra M, Porter R (1998).
Schimck, J.G. (1987) Fact and fantasy in the seduction theory: A historical review Journal of American Psychoanalytic Association 35, 937-65.
Searles HJ (1959a/1965) The effort to drive the other person crazy – an element in the aetiology and psychotherapy of schizophrenia. In Collected Papers on Schizophrenia and Related Subjects. London: Hogarth Press.
Searles HJ (1959b/1965) Oedipal Love in the Countertransference. In Collected Papers on Schizophrenia and Related Subjects. London: Hogarth Press.
Searles HJ (1962/1965) Problems of Psychoanalytic Supervision in Collected Papers

on Schizophrenia and Related Subjects. London: Hogarth Press.
Searles HJ (1979) Countertransference and Related Subjects. New York: International Universities Press.
Selvini Palazzoli M, Boscolo L, Cecchin G, Prata G (1980) Hypothesizing, circularity, neutrality: three guidelines for the conductor of the session. Family Process 19: 3–12.
Selvini Palazzoli M, Cirillo S, Selvini M, Sorrentino AM (1989) Family Games. London: Karnac Books.
Sherwood, R.E. (1950) Roosevelt and Hopkins Vol 1. New York: Bantam.
Smail D (1993) The Origins of Unhappiness. London: Harper Collins.
Spence DP (1982) Narrative Truth and Historical Truth. New York: WW Norton.
Spence DP (1994) The Rhetorical Voice of Psychoanalysis. Cambridge MA: Harvard University Press.
Stern D (1985) The Interpersonal World of the Infant: A View from Psychoanalysis and Developmental Psychology. New York: Basic Books.
Sutherland JD (1987) The status of psychoanalysis. Letter to Times Literary Supplement, 14 August, p. 875.
Suttie I (1935/1988) The Origins of Love and Hate. London: Free Association Books.
Symington N (1986) The analyst's act of freedom as an agent of therapeutic change. In Kohon G (ed.) The British School of Psychoanalysis: the Independant Tradition. New Haven: Yale University Press.
Szasz T (1961) The Myth of Mental Illness. New York: Harper Row.
Thompson M (1998) Mental Hygiene, Liberty and the Roots of Anti-psychiatry in Britain, 1912-1959. In Gijswijt-Hofstra M, Porter R (1998).
Trilling L (1962/1968) The Leavis–Snow controversy. In Beyond Culture: Essays on Literature and Learning. New York: Viking Press.
Vasta R, Haith MH, Miller SA (1992/1995) Child Psychology: The Modern Science. New York: Wiley.
White M (1989) Selected Papers. Adelaide: Dulwich.
Williams B (1993) Shame and Necessity. Berkeley: University of California Press.
Winnicott DWW (1964) The baby as a going concern. In The Child, the Family and the Outside World. Harmondsworth: Penguin.
Winnicott DWW (1965) The Maturational Processes and the Facilitating Environment. London: Hogarth Press.
Winnicott DWW (1971/1974) Playing and Reality. Harmondsworth: Penguin.
Winnicott DWW (1986) Babies and their Mothers. London: Free Association Books.
Wynne LC, Ryckoff IM, Day J, Hirsch S (1958) Pseudo-mutuality in the family relations of schizophrenics. Psychiatry 21: 205–20.
Yalom ID (1996) Lying on the Couch. New York: HarperCollins.

Index

abuse in childhood 66–7
   seduction theory 108–19
academics/students 59–60
Against Therapy (Masson, 1989) 132
aggression 69–70
A Mind that Found Itself (Beers, 1908) 143
analytic attitude 14
   see also ordinariness
anti-psychiatry 141–3
An Unquiet Mind (Jamison, 1995/96) 107
attachment theory 85–6, 103

Balint, M. 19, 29, 84
Bateson, Gregory 2, 20, 55, 120
Beers, Clifford 143
behaviour therapy 15, 94
Bollas, Christopher 79–80
Book of the It (Groddeck, 1923) 99–100
Boss, Medard 11
boundaries 53
Boundary and Space (Davis & Wallbridge, 1983) 52
Bowlby, J. 101–2, 104
Bramley, W. 49
Breuer, Josef 110, 117
British Psycho-analytic Society 2
Byatt, A.S. 83

Cambridge Society for Psychotherapy (the Outfit) 4, 40–7
Case for a Personal Psychotherapy (Lomas, 1981) 92
Cassel Hospital 2, 19
child abuse 66–7
   seduction theory 108–19
Churchill, Ben 34
Clark, Ronald 109
client-centred *see* person-centred approach
Coleridge (poet) 80, 83, 84
Coltart, Nina 56, 79, 86–7
common sense 77
couch (analytic) 54
countertransference *see* transference/countertransference
Critique of Pure Reason (Kant) 76–7
crying 30
Cultivating Intuition (Lomas, 1994) 14, 49, 93

Davis, Kathy 148
death instinct 70
Decent Society, The (Margalit, 1996) 22, 27
dependency issues 37–8
DSM classification 147

Ego and the Id, The (Freud, 1923) 85, 99
ego/superego 65
Esterson, A. 20, 121
evidence-based medicine 147
existential perspective 2, 97
Eysenck, Hans 148

Faith of Counsellors, The (Halmos, 1965) 34
family therapy 120–8
Ferenczi, S. 98
   Lomas on 25, 34, 97
   on transference 8

Fliess, Wilhelm 108–9, 111, 118
free will 103
Freudian Institute 24
Freud, S. 108–19, 130
  on analytic neutrality 54–5
  Lomas on 4–5, 6, 34, 50, 94
  on psychological assertion 63–4
  psychological language of 72–3
  scientific method 101, 104
  seduction theory 108–19
  self-analysis 71–2
  use of metaphor 82–3, 85
  on writers/philosophers 69
friendship 10, 140

Groddeck, G. 99–100
Guild of Psychotherapists 4, 25

Halmos, Paul 34
Hands of the Living God, The (Milner, 1969) 21
Heimann, Paula 19
How Should One Live? (Lomas, 1998) 25–6
humanistic therapy 15
hysteria (Freud on) 110–11

id/ego/superego 65
identifications 75
illusions/truth 98–9
imagination/metaphor 80–8
Independent Group 2
Ingleby, David 48
Institute of Psycho-Analysis 4, 21
International Psychoanalytic Association 69
Interpretation of Dreams (Freud, 1900) 85

Jones, Ernest 53, 71, 108, 111
Jung, C.G. 54, 116–17

Kant 76–7
Kleinian therapists 19, 54
Klein, Melanie 19
Kris, Ernst 119

Lacan, Jacques 61, 69
  Lomas on 33
Laing, R.D. 2, 20, 121, 142–3
Langs, Robert 5

language of psychoanalysis 22, 71
  Lomas' writings 89–95
  ordinary language 62, 63–8, 84, 140
laughter 56
Leaven of Love, The (Forest, 1954) 98
Leavis, F.R. 106
Limits of Interpretation, The (Lomas, 1987) 5, 94
love 98
Lying on the Couch (Yalom, 1996) 145–6, 147

Man Who Mistook His Wife for a Hat, The (Sacks, 1987) 103
Margalit, A. 27
Masson, Jeffrey 109, 132–3
metaphor/imagination 80–8
Milner, Marion 2, 19, 21
Minuchin, S. 125
moral issues 10, 26–7, 28
mother-child relationships 60–1, 105–6
  'still-face' experiments 105, 106
  Winnicottian image 49, 52
motives 73
Myth of Mental Illness, The (Szasz, 1961) 30

Narrative Truth and Historical Truth (Spence, 1982) 84

object relations theory 99, 104
Oedipus complex 109, 117
ordinariness 13–14, 58–9, 62–78, 93, 140
  ordinary language 62, 63–8, 84, 140
Origins of Love and Hate, The (Suttie, 1935) 97
Outfit (Cambridge Society for Psychotherapy) 4, 40–7

Palazzoli, Selvini 126
parent-child relationships 60–1
  see also mother-child relationships
Personal Disorder and Family Life (Lomas, 1998) 3, 139
person-centred approach 53, 55, 135
  Lomas on 50, 55, 56
phylogenetics 116
poetry 22, 80, 93
power of therapist 9–10, 30–1, 51, 140, 148–50

Index

psychoanalysis (Lomas on) 14, 15, 50, 52
   Lomas' own 20
Psychotherapy of Everyday Life (Lomas, 1994) 96, 97, 100
Purity and Danger (Douglas, 1970) 53

Rank, O. 98
Rayner, Eric 55
reframing technique 125
registration issues 132, 136
regression therapy 29–30, 50
relationship *see* therapeutic alliance
religious beliefs 19
"repressed memories" 27
Rogerian approach 135, 145
   Lomas on 2, 4, 50, 55, 56
Rogers, Carl 145
Rycroft, Charles 2, 20, 96

schizophrenia 20, 120–1
scientific method 100–7, 132
   biological reductionism 146–8
Searles, Harold 2, 34–5, 50
   language and style 84
   on supervision 51–2
self-deception 74–6, 119
self-disclosure 23, 54, 97–8
Snow, C.P. 106
Spence, Donald 84
Stern, Daniel 106
Strachey, James 116
students/academics 59–60
superego/ego 65
supervision 49, 51
   Coltart on 86–7
   personal account 48–9, 51
Suttie, Ian 34, 97
Szasz, Thomas 30

therapeutic alliance 5–6, 50–1, 52–3
   authentic relationship 9
   Lomas' approach 56–8, 94–5, 104–5, 133, 140

power of therapist 9–10, 30–1, 51, 140, 148–50
role of metaphor 80–8
rule breaking 56
self-disclosure 23, 54, 97–8
therapists
   dependency issues 37
   narcissistic 30, 94
   need for theory 32
   selection criteria 79, 137
   therapist as person 133–7
   in therapy 25
   see also therapeutic alliance; training issues
training issues 12–15, 24–5
   developing own voice 86
   learning model 50
   Outfit (personal account) 40–7
transference/countertransference 149
   Lomas on 6–8, 32–3, 149
   personal account 39
transmotivation 73
True and False Experience (Lomas, 1973) 1, 4, 8, 48, 49, 98, 100
'true self' concept 11, 29, 80
truth/illusions 98–9

unconscious aims 27–8

Will Therapy (Rank, 1929–31) 98
Winnicott, Clare 101
Winnicott, D.W.W. 49, 52
   on fantasy 88
   on good-enough mothering 60–1
   language and style 84
   Lomas on 97, 2, 19, 29, 34
   on moment of illusion 87
   on scientific method 101
   true self concept 11, 29, 80

Yalom, Irvin 145, 147